# Take
## a box of
# eggs

## Dairy COOKBOOK

# Take
## a box of
# eggs

# Introduction

## EAT THEM

Eggs are one of the most nutritious foods money can buy – they are a natural source of many nutrients including high-quality protein, vitamins and minerals. A medium egg contains less than 80 calories. Eggs are naturally rich in vitamin B2 (riboflavin), vitamin B12 and vitamin D. They also contain vitamin A and a number of other B vitamins including folate, biotin, pantothenic acid and choline. Eggs contain essential minerals and trace elements, including phosphorus, iodine and selenium.

Neither the Food Standards Agency nor the British Heart Foundation recommends a limit on the number of eggs people should eat. Some have had reservations in the past about eating eggs, due to their cholesterol content, but it is now recognised that eating too much saturated fat is more likely to raise blood cholesterol than eating foods rich in dietary cholesterol. Eggs are not high in saturated fat.

The Food Standards Agency recommends that vulnerable groups such as the elderly, very young, sick and pregnant women should eat only eggs that are thoroughly cooked.

## BUY THEM

The majority of eggs available are hens' eggs. They come in various sizes, from small to extra large, and various shades of brown, white and, less commonly, blue. The colour of the shell depends on the breed of the hen. Mixed size eggs are usually a combination of small and medium eggs and tend to be cheaper.

Retailers give various descriptions to describe the way eggs have been farmed:

**Barn eggs** come from chickens kept inside, where there are a maximum of nine birds per square metre.

**Free-range egg** production provides chickens with daytime access to runs covered with vegetation, with a maximum of 2,500 birds per hectare.

**Organic eggs** are from chickens with the same privileges as free-range and are produced according to European laws on organic production. Growth promoters, artificial pesticides, fungicides, herbicides and commercial fertilisers cannot be used in the feed for organic production.

A code is often printed on an egg. The first number refers to the farming method: 0 = **organic**, 1 = **free range**, 2 = **barn**, 3 = **cage**. This is followed by the country of origin and then the farm identification, which is a specific code denoting the actual farm where your eggs were produced.

The **British Lion mark** on egg shells and egg boxes means that the eggs have been produced to the highest standards of food safety. All hens producing Lion Quality eggs must have been vaccinated against Salmonella Enteritidis.

The Lion Code of Practice features stringent feed controls, including a ban on the yolk colourant canthaxanthin. A best-before date and Lion logo must be printed on the shell of Lion Quality eggs as well as on the egg box.

## STORE THEM

Eggs should always be stored in a cool, dry place, ideally in the fridge. Egg shells are porous and can be tainted by other foods, so store eggs apart from other foods, in their egg box.

Eggs can be frozen raw. Cooked eggs don't freeze well. To freeze whole eggs, lightly beat, then add a ¼ tsp of salt or sugar to stabilise, tip into a freezer bag, seal and freeze. Remember to label the bag with the number of eggs and whether they are for sweet or savoury dishes (depending on which condiment has been added). Defrost frozen eggs in the fridge overnight and use them straightaway. As a guide when using frozen eggs, it is useful to remember that 3 tbsp thawed whole egg is equivalent to 1 medium egg. Do not re-freeze eggs once they have been thawed.

Never use eggs after their 'Best Before' date and never use eggs with damaged shells. If the egg is not date stamped, test its freshness by placing it in water. If the egg is stale, it will float and if it sinks, it is fresh. This is because as the egg gets older, the size of the air sac increases, making it float.

## Basic Recipes

# Basic Recipes

## BOIL THEM

### Boiled eggs: method 1 🅥

Time 5½–7 mins. Per portion: 88 Kcal, 7g fat
(1.8g saturated). Serves 1–2

**Eggs** 2

1 Place the eggs in a saucepan of
enough boiling water to cover them
completely.
2 Bring the pan back to the boil and
then simmer gently for 5½–7 minutes
depending on how set you like your
eggs to be.

### Boiled eggs: method 2 🅥

Time 5–6 mins. Per portion: 88 Kcal, 7g fat
(1.8g saturated). Serves 1–2

**Eggs** 2

1 Place the eggs in a saucepan and
cover them with cold water. Bring to
the boil and then simmer gently for
3–5 minutes.

### Hard-boiled eggs 🅥

Time 12 mins. Per portion: 88 Kcal, 7g fat
(1.8g saturated). Serves 1–2

**Eggs** 2

1 Place the eggs in a saucepan of
enough boiling water to cover them
completely. Bring the pan back to the
boil and then simmer gently for 10–12
minutes.
2 Drain the pan and place the eggs under
running cold water to prevent them
from cooking further.
3 Leave to cool, then crack the shells and
peel. Rinse and dry on kitchen paper.

**Cook's tip** Placing the eggs in cold
water after cooking also prevents grey
lines from appearing when shelled.

### Devilled eggs 🅥

Time 20 mins. Per portion: 244 Kcal,
21.8g fat (4.8g saturated). Serves 4

**Eggs** 6 hard-boiled, shelled and cut
lengthways
**Mayonnaise** 4 tbsp
**Powdered mustard** ½ tsp
**White vinegar** ½ tsp
**Salt and freshly ground black pepper**
**Paprika** for sprinkling

1 Remove the egg yolks and mash them
in a small bowl with the remaining
ingredients, except the paprika.
2 Spoon the mixture back into the egg
whites and sprinkle them with some of
the paprika.

## POACH THEM

### Poached eggs 🅥

Time 7 mins. Per portion: 88 Kcal, 7g fat
(1.8g saturated). Serves 2

**White wine vinegar** 1 tbsp
**Eggs** 2

1 Half fill a saucepan with water. Add the
vinegar to the water and bring to the
boil. Crack one of the eggs into a cup
and slide into the water. Repeat with
the second egg.
2 Simmer for 3–5 minutes until lightly set
then lift out with a slotted spoon.

**Cook's tip** To microwave:

1 Put 150ml (¼ pint) of water into a small
bowl with the vinegar.
2 Cook for 1½–2 minutes until boiling.
3 Crack each egg into a cup and slide
into the water. Pierce the yolks and
cook for 20–30 seconds.
4 Allow to stand for 1 minute, then lift out
with a slotted spoon.

**Cook's tip** The vinegar helps the egg
white to coagulate; if your eggs have
been freshly laid, you won't need it.

## Eggs Benedict

Time 20 mins. Per portion: 404 Kcal, 32g fat (17g saturated). Serves 4

**Small slices of bread** 4
**Eggs** 4
**Thin slices of lean ham** 4
**Freshly made Hollandaise sauce** (see page 12)

1 Toast the bread on both sides and poach the eggs (see opposite, below).
2 To serve, top each piece of toast with a slice of ham. Place the drained poached eggs on top, spoon over the Hollandaise sauce and serve.

## FRY THEM

## Fried eggs  Ⓥ

Time 3 mins. Per portion: 108 Kcal, 9g fat (2g saturated). Serves 2

**Vegetable oil** for frying
**Eggs** 2

1 Heat a little oil in a frying pan over a medium heat.
2 Break the eggs into the pan. Baste with the hot oil, tipping the pan if necessary to pool the fat.
3 Cook the eggs until the whites are firm and the yolks cooked to your liking. Remove them from the pan with a fish slice.

## French toast  Ⓥ

Time 5 mins. Per portion: 476 Kcal, 29.9g fat (15.9g saturated). Serves 2

**Eggs** 2
**Milk** 150ml (¼ pint)
**White bread** 4 slices, crusts removed
**Butter** 50g (2oz)

1 Break the eggs into a bowl, add the milk and beat with a fork until mixed.
2 Dip the bread in the egg mixture, coating the slices well.
3 Melt the butter in a frying pan until foaming and fry the bread, turning once, until the slices are golden brown on both sides. Drain on kitchen paper.

**Cinnamon Toast** Follow the recipe for French toast but add 1tsp cinnamon to the butter.

## Pancakes  Ⓥ Ⓕ

Time 25 mins. Per portion: 94 Kcal, 4g fat (1.9g saturated). Makes 8

**Plain flour** 110g (4oz)
**Salt** pinch
**Egg** 1
**Milk** 300ml (½ pint)
**Melted butter or vegetable oil** for frying

1 Sift the flour and salt into a bowl, then break in the egg.
2 Gradually add half the milk, beating to form a smooth batter. Pour in the remaining milk and beat until the mixture is quite smooth.
3 Brush the base of a 20cm (8in) non-stick frying pan with the melted butter or oil and stand over a medium heat.
4 When the pan and fat are hot, pour in 3 tbsp of the batter, tilting the pan to cover the base.
5 Cook the batter until the pancake moves freely, then turn it over and cook until golden.
6 Repeat with the remaining batter until you have 8 pancakes.

## Scrambled eggs 🅥

Time 1½ mins. Per portion: 240 Kcal, 19g fat (7.4g saturated). Serves 1

**Eggs** 2
**Milk** 1 tbsp
**Salt and freshly ground black pepper**
**Butter** 7g (¼oz)

1 Break the eggs into a bowl, add the milk and seasoning and beat with a fork until mixed.
2 Melt the butter in a small saucepan until foaming. Pour in the eggs and stir over a gentle heat with a wooden spoon, moving the eggs from the bottom and sides of saucepan.
3 When the eggs are lightly set remove the pan from the heat. They will continue cooking slightly.

**Cook's tip** To microwave: Prepare the eggs, milk and seasoning as above. Add the butter and cook for about 1½ minutes, stirring frequently, particularly when the eggs begin to set around the edge.

## Plain or French omelette 🅥

Time 5-7 mins. Per portion: 293 Kcal, 26g fat (11.4g saturated). Serves 1

**Eggs** 2
**Salt and freshly ground black pepper**
**Butter** 15g (½oz)

1 Break the eggs into a bowl, add 2 tsp of water and beat lightly together with a fork. Season to taste.
2 Melt the butter in an omelette pan or non-stick frying pan until foaming. Swirl it around to coat the base and sides of the pan.
3 Pour in the beaten eggs. After about 5 seconds, move the edges of the setting omelette to the centre of the pan with a fork. At the same time, tilt the pan quickly in all directions so the uncooked egg flows to the edges.
4 Continue until the mixture is lightly set and the top is slightly soft. Remove from the heat.
5 Fold the omelette in half in the pan and slide out onto a warmed plate.

**Breakfast omelette** Follow the recipe for Plain omelette but fry 1 tbsp each of chopped bacon, mushrooms and onion in a little butter. Add to the beaten eggs just before making the omelette.

## Tortilla 🅥

Time 40 mins. Per portion: 435 Kcal, 28g fat (10.8g saturated). Serves 2

**Butter** 25g (1oz)
**Olive oil** 2 tsp
**Onion** 1 large, peeled and thinly sliced
**Potato** 1 large, boiled, peeled and diced
**Tomatoes** 110g (4oz), chopped
**Red or green peppers** 50g (2oz), deseeded and chopped
**Eggs** 4
**Salt and freshly ground black pepper**

1 Put the butter and oil into a 23cm (9in) non-stick frying pan. When hot and sizzling, add the onion and potato. Fry gently until pale gold, turning often.
2 Add the tomatoes and peppers and fry for a further 2–3 minutes.
3 Beat the eggs lightly with 2 tsp of water. Season to taste then pour into the frying pan over the vegetables. Cook gently until the base is firm.
4 Cook under a preheated hot grill for 1–2 minutes, until just set. Slide the unfolded tortilla onto a warmed plate and cut into two portions.

**Cook's tip** A tortilla is just as good served cold and makes excellent picnic food. After cooking, allow to cool, then cut into wedges and wrap in cling film.

# Egg nog ⓥ

Time 15 mins. Per portion: 193 Kcal, 7.9g fat (03.2g saturated). Serves 3

**Eggs** 2, separated
**Caster sugar** 2 tbsp
**Milk** 600ml (1 pint)
**Ground nutmeg** to serve

1 Whisk the egg yolks and sugar together in a bowl with an electric hand mixer until they are very thick and pale.
2 In a separate bowl and with clean beaters, whisk the egg whites until they form stiff peaks.
3 Bring the milk just up to the boil and whisk into the yolks and sugar. Then quickly stir in the beaten egg whites.
4 Transfer to three glasses and sprinkle with nutmeg. Serve at once.

## BAKE THEM

## Baked eggs ⓥ

Time 17 mins. Per portion: 109 Kcal, 8.8g fat (3.1g saturated). Serves 2

**Butter** 15g (½oz)
**Eggs** 2
**Single cream** 2-4 tbsp (optional)
**Salt and freshly ground black pepper**

1 Preheat the oven to 180°C/350°F/ Gas 4 and grease two 9cm (3½ in) ramekin dishes with the butter.
2 Break an egg into each dish, top with 1 or 2 tbsp of the cream, if using, and season to taste. Bake for 15 minutes until firm and set.

## Quiche Lorraine ⒡

Time 1½ hrs. Per portion: 411 Kcal, 33g fat (18g saturated). Serves 4–5

For the shortcrust pastry
**Plain flour** 225g (8oz)
**Salt** ¼ tsp salt
**Butter** 110g (4oz)
**Cold water** about 3 tbsp

For the filling
**Streaky bacon** 110g (4oz), cut into strips
**Milk** 150ml (¼ pint)
**Single cream** 150ml (¼ pint)
**Eggs** 3, beaten
**Salt and freshly ground black pepper**
**Ground nutmeg** large pinch

1 Preheat the oven to 200°C/400°F/ Gas 6. To make the pastry, sift the flour and salt into a bowl and add the butter. Cut into the flour with a knife, then rub it in with your fingertips until the mixture looks like fine breadcrumbs. Sprinkle some of the water over the crumbs and mix to a stiff crumbly-looking paste with a round-ended knife, adding more water if necessary.
2 If you wish to use a food processor, put all the ingredients, except the water, into the processor. Pulse until the mixture looks like fine breadcrumbs. Then, continuing to pulse, add the water a tablespoon at a time (you may not need all 3 tbsp), until you have a stiff crumbly-looking paste.
3 Draw the pastry together and turn out onto a lightly floured work surface. Knead quickly until smooth and crack-free and then roll it out to line a 20cm (8in) diameter flan tin.
4 For the filling, put a frying pan over a medium heat, add the bacon and fry it lightly in its own fat until soft but not crisp. Drain thoroughly on kitchen paper and place in the base of the pastry case.
5 Heat the milk and cream to just below boiling point and combine with the beaten eggs. Season to taste and add the nutmeg, then pour into the pastry case. Bake in the oven for 10 minutes.
6 Reduce the temperature to 170°C/325°F/Gas 3 and bake for a further 35–45 minutes until set.

## Scotch eggs

Time 1¼ hrs. Per portion: 381 Kcal, 28g fat (9.9g saturated). Serves 6

**Eggs** 6
**White bread**, 2 slices, crusts removed
**Milk** 4 tbsp
**Cumberland sausages** 500g (1lb 2oz)
**Chopped parsley** 2 tbsp
**Ground nutmeg**
**Salt and freshly ground black pepper**
**Streaky bacon** 6 rashers, de-rinded, stretched and cut in half lenghways

1 Preheat the oven to 190°C/375°F/ Gas 5 and have a six-hole deep muffin tin ready.

2 Place the eggs in a saucepan of enough boiling water to cover them completely. Bring the pan back to the boil and then simmer gently for 8 minutes. Drain, then cool in cold water. Shell the eggs and set aside.

3 Put the bread in a large bowl, add the milk and leave for 2 minutes for it to soak in, then mash it down with your hand – this makes it easier to mix with the rest of the ingredients.

4 Split the skins on the sausages and put the meat into the bowl with the soaked bread and discard the skins. Add the parsley, a good grating of nutmeg and seasoning. Work everything together with your hand. Divide the mixture into six balls, then flatten them to make rounds.

5 Stand a boiled egg in the middle of each round, pointed end up, and work the meat up around the egg to form a smooth, even layer, sealing the egg completely.

6 Put each egg in a hole in the muffin tin then criss-cross two pieces of bacon over the top, tucking in the loose ends.

7 Bake for about 35 minutes until golden. Leave the eggs to stand for 5 minutes in the tin and then run a knife around the edge to get them out. Drain on kitchen paper and serve warm or cold with salad and mustard or mayonnaise.

**Cook's tip** You'll find it easier to mould the meat around the egg if your hands are wet, not floured.

## Cheese soufflé

Time 1¼ hrs. Per portion: 356 Kcal, 26g fat (14.7g saturated). Serves 4

**Butter** 50g (2oz)
**Plain flour** 50g (2oz)
**Milk** 300ml (½ pint), warmed
**Cheddar cheese** 110g (4oz), grated
**Mustard** 1 tsp
**Salt and freshly ground black pepper**
**Worcestershire sauce** ¼ tsp
**Egg yolks** 3
**Egg whites** 4

1 Preheat the oven to 190°C/375°F/ Gas 5 and grease a 1.5 litre (2½ pint) soufflé dish (or similar straight-sided, heatproof dish).
2 Melt the butter in a saucepan and add the flour. Cook for 2 minutes without browning, stirring all the time.
3 Using a whisk, slowly whisk in the warm milk. Continue whisking gently until the sauce thickens, boils and is smooth.
4 Simmer the sauce for about 2 minutes. It should eventually be quite thick and leave the sides of the pan clean.
5 Remove the pan from the heat and leave the sauce to cool slightly. Beat in the cheese, mustard, seasoning, Worcestershire sauce and egg yolks.
6 In a bowl, whisk the egg whites with an electric hand whisk until they form stiff peaks. Gently fold them into the sauce mixture with a large metal spoon.
7 Transfer to the prepared soufflé dish and bake for about 50 minutes until the soufflé is well risen and golden.
8 Remove from the oven and serve at once. It is vital not to open the oven door while the soufflé is baking or it will collapse.

**Ham soufflé** Follow the recipe for Cheese soufflé but omit the cheese. Before beating in the egg yolks, add 110g (4oz) of finely chopped ham.

## Meringues Ⓥ Ⓕ

Time 2¾ hrs. Per meringue: 35 Kcal, 0g fat. Makes 16

**Egg whites** 2
**Pinch of cream of tartar** (optional)
**Caster sugar** 110g (4oz)
**Granulated sugar** 25g (1oz)

1 Preheat the oven to 110°C/225°F/ Gas ¼ and brush a large baking sheet with oil. Cover it with a double thickness of greaseproof or non-stick baking paper. Do not brush the paper with more oil.
2 Put the egg whites into a clean dry bowl and add the cream of tartar, if using. Whisk with an electric hand whisk until the whites form soft peaks. Add half the caster sugar. Continue whisking until the meringue is shiny and stands in firm peaks.
3 Add the remaining caster sugar and whisk once more until the meringue is very stiff and silky-looking. Gently fold in the granulated sugar.
4 Pipe or spoon 16 rounds or ovals onto the prepared sheet and bake for 2½ hours or until crisp and firm.
5 Transfer to a wire cooling rack and leave until cold.

**Coffee meringues** Follow the recipe for meringues but add 2 tsp instant coffee powder with the granulated sugar.

## Macaroons ⓥ ⒡

Time 50 mins. Per macaroon: 93 Kcal, 4g fat
(0.3g saturated). Makes 18

**Egg whites** 2, plus a little extra for brushing
**Ground almonds** 110g (4oz)
**Caster sugar** 225g (8oz)
**Ground rice** 15g (½oz)
**Vanilla extract** ½ tsp
**Almond extract** ½ tsp
**Blanched almonds** 9, split in half
**Rice paper** to cover 2 baking sheets

1 Preheat the oven to 170°C/325°F/
  Gas 3 and grease two baking sheets,
  then line them with rice paper.
2 In a bowl, whisk the egg whites with an
  electric hand whisk until they are foamy
  but not stiff. Add the ground almonds,
  sugar, ground rice, vanilla and almond
  extract. Mix together well.
3 Pipe or spoon 18 mounds of the
  mixture, spaced well apart, onto the
  baking sheets. Brush with egg white
  and top with an almond half.
4 Bake for 20–25 minutes, or until pale
  gold. Remove from the oven and leave
  to cool for 5 minutes. Carefully remove
  the rice paper from the edges and then
  rest on a wire cooling rack. Store in an
  airtight container when cold.

## SAUCE THEM

## Hollandaise sauce ⓥ

Time 20 mins. Per portion: 329 Kcal, 35g fat
(20.8g saturated). Serves 6

**Lemon juice** 1 tsp
**White wine vinegar** 1 tsp
**Peppercorns** 3
**Bay leaf** ½ small
**Egg yolks** 4 large
**Butter** 225g (8oz), softened
**Salt and freshly ground black pepper**

1 Put the lemon juice and vinegar
  with 1 tbsp of cold water and the
  peppercorns and bay leaf into a
  saucepan. Boil gently until the liquor
  is reduced by half. Leave until cold,
  then strain.
2 Put the egg yolks and reduced vinegar
  liquor into a basin standing over a
  saucepan of gently simmering water.
  Whisk until it is thick and foamy, then
  gradually add the butter, a tiny piece
  at a time. Continue whisking until each
  piece has been absorbed by the sauce.
  Season to taste and serve.

**Mousseline sauce** Follow the recipe
for Hollandaise sauce, above, and stir in
3 tbsp lightly whipped double cream just
before serving.

## Blender hollandaise sauce ⓥ

Time 15 mins. Per portion: 230 Kcal, 25g fat
(14.8g saturated). Serves 4

**Egg yolks** 3 large
**Lemon juice** 1 tbsp
**Salt and freshly ground black pepper**
**Butter** 110g (4oz), melted

1 Place the egg yolks, lemon juice
  and seasoning in a blender or food
  processor. Cover and pulse for a few
  seconds to mix.
2 Gradually pour the hot, melted butter
  into the blender while processing at a
  high speed.
3 Blend until the sauce is thick and light,
  and serve.

## Mayonnaise ⓥ

Time 20 mins. Per tbsp: 131 Kcal, 14.3g fat
(2.1g saturated). Makes about 300ml (½ pint)

**Egg yolks** 2 large
**Mustard powder, salt and sugar** ½ tsp of
each
**Freshly ground black pepper**
**Olive oil** 300ml (½ pint)
**White wine vinegar or lemon juice** 2 tbsp
**Hot water** 1 tbsp
All ingredients should be at room temperature.

1 Place the egg yolks, mustard, salt, sugar and pepper in a bowl and beat until smooth.
2 Beating more quickly, very slowly add 150ml (¼ pint) of the oil, a drop at a time, and continue beating until the mayonnaise is very thick.
3 Stir in 1 tbsp of the vinegar or lemon juice. Beat in the remaining oil gradually, about 2 tsp at a time. When all the oil has been added, stir in the remaining vinegar or lemon juice and 1 tbsp of hot water (this helps prevent separation).
4 Adjust the seasoning to taste and transfer the mayonnaise to a covered container. It will keep in a refrigerator for up to 2 weeks.

**Thousand island dressing** Follow the recipe above for mayonnaise. Stir 4 tbsp double cream, 4 tsp tomato ketchup, ½ tsp chilli sauce, 2 tbsp finely chopped stuffed olives, 2 tsp finely chopped onion, 1 tbsp finely chopped green pepper, 1 hard-boiled egg, shelled and finely chopped, and 3 tbsp chopped parsley into the mayonnaise after adding the hot water.

**Aioli (garlic mayonnaise)** Follow the recipe above for mayonnaise. Stir 1 crushed garlic clove into the mayonnaise after adding the hot water.

**Tartare sauce** Follow the recipe above for mayonnaise. Stir 1 tbsp each finely chopped capers and parsley and 2 tbsp finely chopped gherkins into the mayonnaise after adding the hot water.

## Real custard ⓥ

Time 20 mins plus standing time. Per portion: 90 Kcal, 5g fat (1.7g saturated). Serves 4–6

**Milk** 300ml (½ pint)
**Vanilla pod** 1, cut in half lengthways

**Egg yolks** 4 large
**Caster sugar** 25g (1oz)

1 Reserve 3 tbsp of the milk. Place the remaining milk and the vanilla pod in a saucepan and gently heat until the milk is almost boiling. Remove the pan from the heat and leave it to stand for 15 minutes.
2 Place the egg yolks, sugar and reserved milk in a bowl and beat until they are thick and creamy.
3 Remove the vanilla pod from the milk and pour the milk onto the egg mixture.
4 Strain the mixture into a heavy-based saucepan and cook, stirring, until the custard thinly coats the back of a wooden spoon (about the thickness of single cream).
5 Pour into a cold jug and serve hot or cold. The sauce thickens on cooling.

RECIPE NOTES

Use medium or large eggs, unless specified.

Recipes with ⓥ symbol are suitable for vegetarians if using vegetarian cheese and/or yogurt.

The very young, pregnant or elderly should not eat recipes using raw or lightly cooked eggs.

Recipes using nuts are not suitable for young children or for those with an allergic reaction to nuts.

Calories, fat and saturated fat have been calculated by portion or item.

# Toasts
# &
# Snacks

Time required
**8 mins**

Per portion
**311 Kcal**
**15.6g fat**
**(7.4g saturated)**

# Luxury egg & cress sandwiches

Makes 4  Ⓥ

**Eggs** 4, hard-boiled, shelled and cooled

**Boursin cheese with black pepper** 50g (2oz) or to taste

**Light mayonnaise** 3–4 tbsp

**Salt** a pinch (optional)

**Wholemeal bread** 8 slices or 4 soft oatmeal rolls

**Salad cress** a punnet

1   Cut the hard-boiled eggs in half, tip into a bowl and mash with a fork until the whites are chopped into small pieces.

2   Add the Boursin cheese and enough mayonnaise to make a thick spreadable filling. Season with salt, if wished.

3   Spread the filling over one side of each slice of bread or roll. Scatter half the bread with snipped salad cress and pop the remaining bread on top to make four sandwiches. Cut each sandwich into four triangles and serve, garnished with a little extra salad cress, if wished.

**Cook's tip** This egg filling also makes a brilliant topping for bridge rolls or an easy starter – just add to ready-made blinis and top with thin strips of smoked salmon. You may also prefer to garnish with wild rocket instead of salad cress.

Scan with Smartphone for shopping list

Time required
**25 mins**

Per portion
**426 Kcal**
**23.5g fat**
**(7.1g saturated)**

# Mexican-style scrambled egg wrap

Serves 4 **Ⓥ**

**Olive oil** 2 tbsp

**Red pepper** 1, deseeded and sliced

**Green pepper** 1, deseeded and sliced

**Spring onions** 3, trimmed and sliced

**Sun-dried tomatoes in olive oil** 6, drained and chopped

**Eggs** 6, beaten

**Salt and freshly ground black pepper**

**Butter** 25g (1oz)

**Soft flour tortillas** 4, warmed

1. Heat the olive oil in a large frying pan, preferably non-stick. Add the peppers and cook gently for 5 minutes, until softened. Then add the spring onions and sun-dried tomatoes and heat through. Remove from the pan and set aside.

2. Season the eggs. Add the butter to the frying pan, allow it to melt until sizzling hot, and then mix in the eggs and stir gently, but quickly, until the eggs are lightly scrambled.

3. Divide the fried vegetables between the tortillas and top with the scrambled eggs. Roll them up and serve at once.

Scan with Smartphone for shopping list

Time required
**7 mins**

Per portion
**722 Kcal
51g fat
(24.2g saturated)**

# Scrambled eggs with smoked salmon

Serves 2

**Butter** 75g (3oz), softened
**Tomato purée** 2 tsp
**Chopped dill** 2 tbsp, plus a few fronds to garnish
**Capers** 2–3 tbsp, drained and roughly chopped
**Freshly ground black pepper**

**Mediterranean-style bread with olives** 4 slices, about 2cm (¾in) thick
**Eggs** 4, beaten
**Smoked salmon slices** 100g packet, cut into thin strips
**Beefsteak tomato** 1, deseeded and diced, to garnish (optional)

1   Put 50g (2oz) of the butter into a small bowl, then add the tomato purée, chopped dill and capers. Season with black pepper, then mix well together and set aside. Toast the bread and keep it warm.

2   Melt the remaining butter in a small saucepan (preferably non-stick), add the eggs and half of the salmon strips. Then cook over a moderate heat, stirring continuously, until the eggs are softly scrambled – taking care not to overcook, as they will become dry.

3   Spread the toasted bread with the tomato butter and put onto two serving plates. Spoon the scrambled eggs on top, garnish with the remaining strips of salmon, dill and the chopped tomato, if using. Add a good grinding of black pepper and serve at once.

**Cook's tip** For quick assembly, prepare all the ingredients before starting to cook and toast the bread while scrambling the eggs.

Scan with Smartphone for shopping list

Time required
**30 mins**

Per portion
**298 Kcal**
**21.6g fat**
**(7.7g saturated)**

# Piperade

Serves 4 Ⓥ

**Olive oil** 1 tbsp

**Onions** 350g (12oz), peeled and chopped

**Green peppers** 2, deseeded and cut into strips

**Tomatoes** 450g (1lb), chopped

**Chopped basil** 1 tbsp, plus tiny leaves to garnish

**Salt and freshly ground black pepper**

**Eggs** 6

**Double cream** 4 tbsp

**Toasted rustic bread** to serve (optional)

1   Heat the oil in a frying pan and gently fry the onions until they are soft but not brown. Add the peppers and cook slowly with the onion until soft.

2   Add the tomatoes with the basil and seasoning. Cover and simmer for 20 minutes or until most of the liquid has evaporated.

3   Break the eggs into a bowl, add the cream and beat lightly with a fork. Pour the eggs over the vegetable mixture and cook, stirring, until the eggs are scrambled. Divide between four warmed bowls and serve with the basil leaves scattered over the top and slices of toast, if using.

Scan with Smartphone for shopping list

Time required
**30 mins**

Per portion
**386 Kcal**
**21.6g fat**
**(11.2g saturated)**

# Creamy cherry tomato & mushroom toasts

Serves 4

**Cherry tomatoes** 500g (1lb 2oz)

**Spring onions** 4, trimmed and finely chopped

**Eggs** 2 large

**Plain flour** 2 tbsp

**Single cream** 142ml pot

**Salt and freshly ground black pepper**

**Mature Cheddar cheese** 50g (2oz), finely grated

**Butter** 25g (1oz), melted

**Flat mushrooms** 4 large, wiped

**Bread** 4 chunky slices

**Parmesan cheese** 2 tbsp, grated (optional)

1   Preheat the oven to 190°C/375°F/Gas 5. Butter a shallow ovenproof dish and put the tomatoes and spring onions in it. Break the eggs into a bowl and lightly whisk, then whisk in the flour, cream and seasoning. Stir in the Cheddar cheese. Pour the mixture over the onions and tomatoes in the dish and bake in the oven for about 20 minutes until just set.

2   Brush the butter all over the mushrooms and place them stalk-sides down in a small roasting tin. Bake for 15 minutes, turning them over halfway through cooking. Toast the bread.

3   To serve, place a slice of toast on each of four plates. Cut the savoury custard into four and place a wedge on each piece of toast and then add a mushroom. Scatter the Parmesan cheese on top, if using. A crisp green salad would go well with this.

**Cook's tip** For a vegetarian version simply omit the Parmesan.

Scan with Smartphone
for shopping list

Time required
**20 mins**

Per portion
**652 Kcal**
**51.3g fat**
**(21.6g saturated)**

# Muffins with mushrooms & scrambled eggs

Serves 4  Ⓥ

**Olive oil** 3–4 tbsp

**Spring onions** 4, trimmed and sliced

**Mushrooms** 400g (14oz) mixture of small flat, closed cup and chestnut, wiped, trimmed and sliced

**Chopped parsley** 2 tbsp, plus extra to serve (optional)

**Eggs** 8

**Double cream** 125ml (4fl oz)

**Salt and freshly ground black pepper**

**Butter** 50g (2oz)

**Cheddar and black pepper muffins** 4, halved and toasted

1   Heat the oil in a large non-stick frying pan, add the spring onions and cook for a minute or so, stirring. Add the mushrooms and continue cooking over a high heat, stirring frequently, for about 5 minutes or until the onions are cooked and turning golden. Add the parsley for the last minute of cooking.

2   Meanwhile, beat together the eggs and cream with salt and pepper. Melt the butter in a separate large non-stick pan and, when foaming, add the egg mix. Cook over a gentle heat, stirring, until softly scrambled.

3   Pop the hot toasted muffins onto warmed plates. Spoon over the mushrooms, top with the scrambled eggs and serve at once with extra chopped parsley to garnish, if using.

**Cook's tip** Use any combination of your favourite fresh mushrooms and, if you like onions, add a few more chopped spring onions to cook with the mushrooms.

Scan with Smartphone for shopping list

Time required
**25 mins**

Per portion
**354 Kcal**
**21.8g fat**
**(4.6g saturated)**

# Asparagus with poached eggs

Serves 4

**Asparagus spears** 12, washed

**Olive oil** 4 tbsp

**Rustic bread or ciabatta** 4 large or 8 small slices

**Parma or Serrano ham** 6 slices, cut in half widthways

**Wine or cider vinegar** a dash

**Eggs** 4

**Salt and freshly ground black pepper**

1   Preheat the oven to 200°C/400°F/Gas 6. Break the ends off the asparagus stalks where they naturally snap. Put the asparagus on a baking sheet, drizzle with 1 tbsp of the oil and rub it over the spears with your hands. Bake for 5 minutes.

2   Meanwhile, drizzle the rest of the oil over the slices of bread. When cooked, take the asparagus out of the oven and wrap half a piece of Parma or Serrano ham around each stalk and put back on the baking sheet. Place the bread alongside. Bake for 10 minutes until the ham starts to go crispy, but do not overcook.

3   While the asparagus and bread are baking, bring a wide saucepan of water to the boil and add a dash of vinegar. Break in the eggs, one at a time, and let them poach over a gentle heat for 3–4 minutes, depending on how you like them.

4   Arrange the baked bread and roasted asparagus on four warmed plates. Remove the poached eggs from the saucepan with a draining spoon and place on top. Season and serve at once.

**Cook's tip** Adding vinegar to the egg poaching water helps the eggs to coagulate more quickly – wine, cider or rice vinegar is preferable to malt vinegar.

Scan with Smartphone for shopping list

Time required
**15 mins**

Per portion
**669 Kcal**
**49g fat**
**(24.8g saturated)**

# Croque-monsieur

Serves 2

**Multigrain bread** 4 slices

**Butter** for spreading, softened

**Gruyère cheese** 75g (3oz), grated

**Cooked ham** 4 thin slices, trimmed of fat

**Eggs** 2, beaten

**Butter** 25g (1oz)

**Sunflower oil** 1 tbsp

**Mixed salad** to serve (optional)

1   Lightly spread the slices of bread with butter. Scatter two slices with the grated cheese, followed by the ham. Pop the other slices on top to make a sandwich.

2   Press down to stick them together and trim the crusts if wished (but it is not really necessary). Make sure you tuck any overlapping ham into the sandwich before trimming or you will waste it. Cut each Croque Monsieur into four squares.

3   Lightly beat the eggs together and pour into a shallow dish. Dip both sides of the small sandwiches into the egg mixture.

4   Heat the butter and oil together in a large non-stick frying pan. Add the sandwiches and cook for about 3 minutes on each side until golden and crisp and the cheese is starting to ooze from the sides. Serve at once with a mixed salad, if using.

**Cook's tip** Once you have the basic recipe, try using different hard cheeses such as mature Cheddar or Emmental in the filling. You can cut the sandwiches into triangles rather than squares and if you add a fried egg on top of each portion of four mini sandwiches, the French call it Croque-madame.

Scan with Smartphone for shopping list

# Vegetarian

33

Time required
**20 mins**

Per portion
**448 Kcal**
**30.4g fat**
**(5.4g saturated)**

# Easy gado gado salad

Serves 4  **V**

## For the dressing

**Salted peanuts** 50g (2oz)

**Red chilli** ½, halved and deseeded

**Toasted sesame oil** 1 tbsp

**Onion** 1 small (the size of a shallot), peeled and quartered

**Garlic** 1 clove, peeled

**Soy sauce** 1 tbsp

**Lime** 1, juice only

**Sunflower oil** 3–4 tbsp

## For the salad

**Sunflower oil** 2 tbsp

**Onions** 2, peeled and thinly sliced

**Potatoes** 450g (1lb) (about 2), scrubbed and cut into chunks, then boiled and cooled

**Eggs** 4, hard-boiled, shelled and quartered

**Beansprouts** 110g (4oz), blanched and drained

**Fine green beans** 110g (4oz), trimmed, blanched and drained

**Baby spinach** 75g (3oz), washed and drained

**Cucumber** 10cm (4in) piece, cut into strips

1   To make the dressing, put everything except the sunflower oil together with 5 tbsp of water in a mini blender and purée until smooth. Tip the sauce into a small saucepan and bring to the boil. Lower the heat, cover and simmer very gently for 5 minutes, stirring occasionally. Then remove from the heat and leave to cool. Gradually whisk in the oil to make a thick dressing.

2   For the salad, heat the oil in a heavy-based frying pan over a medium heat. Add the onions and cook slowly for about 10 minutes until they start to turn a deep golden colour. Remove from the heat and drain off any excess oil.

3   Cut the cooked potatoes into bite-sized pieces. Arrange the potatoes, eggs, beansprouts, beans, spinach and cucumber in layers in a large salad bowl. Scatter with the crispy onions, pour over the dressing and toss together gently. Serve at once.

Scan with Smartphone
for shopping list

**Cook's tip** To blanch the beansprouts, plunge into boiling water for just one minute; the green beans will need three minutes in boiling water.

Time required
10 mins

Per portion
434 Kcal
36.1g fat
(17.2g saturated)

# Brie & chive omelette

Serves 2  Ⓥ

**Eggs** 4
**Salt and freshly ground black pepper**
**Chives** small bunch
**Butter** a knob

**Brie or Camembert** 110g (4oz), rind left on
**Potato wedges and mixed salad** to serve (optional)

1 Break the eggs into a bowl and lightly beat with a fork until just mixed. Add seasoning and use scissors to snip the chives straight in – you are aiming for about 4 tbsp of the chopped chives.

2 Heat a frying pan, add the butter and when it sizzles, shake the pan to swirl the butter around. Reduce the heat a little and pour half of the eggs into the pan. Move the pan around so the eggs are spread out evenly and cook for 1–2 minutes until the omelette is beginning to set.

3 Snip the cheese with scissors in rough cubes over the omelette. Leave on a low heat for 30 seconds, then, using a spatula, fold one-third of the omelette to the middle, then the other third over and slide it onto a plate. Repeat to make a second omelette. Serve with the potato wedges and mixed salad, if using.

Scan with Smartphone for shopping list

Time required
**30 mins**

Per portion
**321 Kcal**
**17.7g fat**
**(4.2g saturated)**

# Sweet potato & pepper Spanish omelette

Serves 3  Ⓥ

**Sweet potato** 1 large, peeled, cut in half lengthways and then into 5mm (¼in) slices

**Vegetable oil** 1 tbsp

**Red pepper** 1, deseeded and cut into thin slices

**Garlic** 2 cloves, peeled and crushed

**Eggs** 6, beaten

**Salt and freshly ground black pepper**

**Chopped parsley** 2 tbsp

**Chopped coriander** 2 tbsp

1   Place the sweet potato in a saucepan, cover with water, bring to the boil and cook for about 5 minutes until just tender. Drain well.

2   Heat the oil in a frying pan and gently fry the pepper and garlic for about 5 minutes until softened. Add the sweet potato slices, and cook, stirring, for a further minute.

3   Pack the vegetables evenly over the base of the frying pan and pour in the eggs and plenty of seasoning. Cook over a gentle heat for about 10 minutes, mixing the cooked egg from the edge of the pan into the centre, until the egg is set all over.

4   Preheat the grill to hot, and place the omelette under the grill, protecting the frying pan handle if necessary, to cook for 2–3 minutes to brown the top.

5   Serve hot or cold, straight from the pan, cut into wedges, and sprinkled generously with the chopped herbs.

Scan with Smartphone for shopping list

Time required
**15–18 mins**

Per portion
**351 Kcal**
**29g fat**
**(12.2g saturated)**

# Easy cheesy soufflé omelette

Serves 2  Ⓥ

**Eggs** 4
**Snipped chives** 2 tbsp
**Salt and freshly ground black pepper**

**Camembert cheese** 110g (4oz), chopped
**Sunflower oil** 2 tsp
**Roasted vegetables** to serve (optional)

1   It is easier to make one omelette at a time – unless you are lucky enough to have two smallish non-stick frying pans. Separate two of the eggs into two bowls. Beat the egg yolks with half the chives and season with salt and pepper. Divide the chopped cheese into four portions and stir one of the portions into the egg yolks.

2   Whisk the egg whites with an electric hand whisk until they form stiff peaks, then gently fold into the cheesy egg mix with a metal spoon. Preheat the grill to hot.

3   Heat 1 tsp of the oil in a non-stick frying pan and add the egg mix. Cook until the omelette is just starting to turn golden underneath. Then scatter with another portion of cheese. Pop the pan under the grill and continue cooking until the cheese has melted and the omelette is puffed and only just set.

4   Carefully tip the omelette onto a serving plate, folding it in half as you do so. Repeat with the remaining mix to make the second omelette. Serve with roasted vegetables, if using.

**Cook's tip** If not cooking for vegetarians, use Taleggio cheese instead of Camembert.

Scan with Smartphone for shopping list

Time required
**35 mins**

Per portion
**500 Kcal**
**30.5g fat**
**(11.2g saturated)**

# Potato, thyme & blue cheese frittata

Serves 3 **Ⓥ**

**Potatoes** 500g (1lb 2oz), cut into bite-sized pieces

**Fine green beans** 110g (4oz), trimmed and halved

**Asparagus tips** 100g packet, trimmed

**Eggs** 6

**Salt and freshly ground black pepper**

**Lemon thyme** a couple of sprigs, leaves plucked

**Olive oil** 2 tbsp

**Blacksticks Blue cheese** 110g (4oz), chopped or crumbled into small pieces

**Mixed salad and ciabatta** to serve (optional)

1   Bring a saucepan of water to the boil, add the potatoes, lower the heat and cook the potatoes at a simmer for 15–20 minutes until tender. Drain the potatoes and set aside. Plunge the green beans and asparagus tips in a separate saucepan of boiling water for 2 minutes, then drain them, too.

2   Beat together the eggs with salt and pepper and the thyme leaves.

3   Heat the oil in a large non-stick frying pan. Add the potatoes and cook for 5 minutes or until the potatoes are starting to colour, stirring every now and then. Don't worry if the potatoes start to break up. Then add the beans and asparagus and cook for a further 1–2 minutes, stirring frequently.

4   Preheat the grill to hot. Pour the egg mixture into the frying pan, over the vegetables, and cook the frittata for 3–5 minutes, or until it is just set on the bottom. Dot the cheese on top of the frittata and finish cooking under the grill until the egg is just set. Watch the omelette carefully so the cheese doesn't overcook.

5   Loosen the edges of the frittata with a knife and turn out onto a serving plate. Cut into wedges and serve hot with a mixed salad and warm ciabatta, if using.

43

Scan with Smartphone for shopping list

Time required
**45 mins**

Per portion
**520 Kcal**
**42.9g fat**
**(19.6g saturated)**

# Goat's cheese soufflés with a walnut salad

Serves 4  **V**

**Butter** 75g (3oz)

**Parmesan-style vegetarian cheese** 50g (2oz), finely grated

**Plain flour** 50g (2oz)

**Full fat milk** 300ml (½ pint)

**Rindless goat's cheese** 100g (3½oz), broken into pieces

**Eggs** 4, separated

**Salt and freshly ground black pepper**

**Ground nutmeg** a couple of generous pinches

**Mixed salad leaves** 50g (2oz), such as watercress, baby spinach and rocket

**Walnut pieces** 25g (1oz)

**Olive oil** 2 tbsp

**Lime** 1, juice only

1   Melt 25g (1oz) of the butter and use it to grease four 200ml (7fl oz) soufflé dishes. Then sprinkle with some of the Parmesan-style cheese. This gives the soufflés something to stick to as they rise. Set the dishes on a baking sheet.

2   Melt the remaining butter in a large saucepan, add the flour and mix well. Remove the pan from the heat and gradually add the milk, whisking well after each addition. Then return the pan to the heat and bring the sauce to the boil, whisking all the time. Continue cooking for about 1 minute, still whisking, until you have a smooth thick sauce. Remove the pan from the heat and leave to cool for 10 minutes. Preheat the oven to 200°C/400°F/Gas 6.

3   Beat in the goat's cheese and remaining Parmesan-style cheese. Then beat in the egg yolks. Season with salt, pepper and nutmeg.

4   Whisk the egg whites with an electric hand whisk until they form stiff peaks. Fold one-third into the cheese sauce with a metal spoon, then gently fold in the rest. Spoon the mix into the prepared dishes and bake for 15–20 minutes or until golden and well risen.

Scan with Smartphone for shopping list

5   Drizzle the salad and walnuts with oil and lime juice and serve as soon as the soufflés come out of the oven.

Time required
**20 mins**

Per portion
**397 Kcal**
**19g fat**
**(8.8g saturated)**

# Glamorgan sausages with tomato salad

Serves 4 **V** **F**

**Breadcrumbs** 175g (6oz)

**Caerphilly cheese** 110g (4oz), grated

**Leek** 1 small, trimmed, washed and very finely chopped

**Chopped parsley** 1 tbsp

**Mustard powder** ½ tsp

**Salt and freshly ground black pepper**

**Eggs** 2, 1 separated

**Milk** 4 tbsp (optional)

**Plain flour** 2 tbsp

**Vegetable oil** 1 tbsp

**Butter** 15g (½oz)

**Tomatoes** sliced, to serve

**Parsley** to garnish

1 In a large bowl combine the breadcrumbs, cheese, leek, parsley and mustard. Season to taste. Add 1 whole egg and 1 egg yolk and mix thoroughly. If necessary, add enough milk to bind the mixture together.

2 Divide the mixture into eight and shape into sausages about 10cm (4in) long.

3 On a large plate, beat the remaining egg white with a fork until frothy. Place the sausages on the plate and brush the egg white all over them, until evenly coated. Roll the sausages in the flour.

4 Heat the oil and butter in a frying pan and fry the sausages for 5–10 minutes, turning occasionally, until golden brown. Serve hot or cold on a bed of sliced tomatoes and with a sprig of parsley.

**Cook's tip** For a vegetarian main meal, serve with potato wedges and a large salad.

Time required
**35 mins**

Per portion
**350 Kcal**
**17g fat**
**(3.7g saturated)**

# Baked rice-stuffed peppers

Serves 4  **V**

**Red peppers** 4 large, halved and deseeded
**Olive oil** 1 tbsp
**Egg-fried rice** 250g carton
**Sweetcorn** 198g can, drained
**Frozen peas** 50g (2oz)

**Chopped coriander** 1 tbsp
**Salt and freshly ground black pepper**
**Eggs** 8
**Soy sauce** to serve, optional

1   Preheat the oven to 200°C/400°F/Gas 6. Place the peppers on a baking sheet and brush them on the inside and cut edges with the olive oil. Place the baking sheet in the oven and bake the peppers for 15 minutes.

2   Meanwhile, mix together the egg-fried rice, sweetcorn, peas, coriander and seasoning.

3   Remove the peppers from the oven and spoon the rice mixture into the cavities, pressing the mixture down well and hollowing it slightly in the centre. Break an egg into each pepper and grind a little black pepper on top of each one.

4   Return the baking sheet with the peppers to the oven and bake for a further 12–15 minutes, or until the eggs have just set.

5   Remove the peppers from the oven and serve two halves per person, with soy sauce, if using, to drizzle over the rice.

**Cook's tip** When cutting the peppers in half, cut through the stalks as the peppers look more stylish with the stalks left on them.

Scan with Smartphone
for shopping list

Time required
**1 hr 20 mins**

Per portion
**780 Kcal**
**43.2g fat**
**(20.3g saturated)**

# Eggs au gratin

Serves 2 Ⓥ

**Eggs** 4

**Butter** 25g (1oz)

**Spring onions** 4 large, trimmed and thinly sliced

**Plain flour** 25g (1oz)

**Milk** 300ml (½ pint)

**Double Gloucester or Cheddar cheese** 75g (3oz), grated

**Salt and freshly ground black pepper**

**Tomatoes** 2–3, sliced

**White breadcrumbs** 3 rounded tbsp

**Rolled oats** 3 rounded tbsp

1   Preheat the oven to 180°C/350°F/Gas 4. Put the eggs into a small saucepan, cover with cold water, bring to the boil and boil gently for 10 minutes. Remove the eggs from the pan and cool in cold water until cold. Shell the eggs, then cut them in half lengthways and arrange, cut sides down, in two lightly buttered, shallow 450ml (¾ pint) ovenproof dishes.

2   To make the sauce, melt the butter in a saucepan, add the spring onions and cook gently for 2–3 minutes until softened, but not browned.

3   Stir the flour into the butter and onions, add the milk and bring slowly up to the boil, stirring continuously until the sauce thickens. Add two-thirds of the cheese and stir well until the cheese melts. Season to taste.

4   Pour the sauce evenly over the eggs and arrange the sliced tomatoes over the top. Mix together the breadcrumbs, oats and remaining cheese and sprinkle evenly over the sauce. Bake in the oven for 30–40 minutes, until golden brown and bubbling hot.

**Cook's tip** This dish may be prepared well in advance of baking. Cool, then cover and refrigerate. Allow extra time when reheating.

51

Scan with Smartphone for shopping list

Time required
**1 hr, + standing**

Per portion
**699 Kcal**
**47g fat**
**(26.1g saturated)**

# Bread & cheese bake

Serves 2 **V** **F**

**Wholemeal bread with pumpkin seeds or multigrain** 4 slices

**Butter** 40g (1½oz), softened

**Mature Cheddar cheese** 110g (4oz), grated

**Spring onions** 4, trimmed and finely sliced

**Mixed dried herbs** ¼ tsp

**Eggs** 2

**Milk** 300ml (½ pint)

**Cayenne pepper or paprika** for sprinkling

1  Spread the bread with the butter and cut each slice in two, lengthways.

2  Butter two 500ml (18fl oz) shallow baking dishes. Arrange overlapping slices of the bread across the dishes and sprinkle with the cheese, onions and herbs.

3  Break the eggs into a bowl, add the milk and whisk together. Then carefully pour over the bread in each dish. Place the dishes on a baking tray and leave to stand for 30 minutes. Meanwhile, heat the oven to 190°C/375°F/Gas 5.

4  Bake the puddings for 20–25 minutes, until golden brown and set. Sift with cayenne or paprika and serve while piping hot.

**Cook's tip** This bread and cheese pudding is quite rich, so serve simply with a mixed leaf salad sprinkled with seasoned rice vinegar.

53

Time required
**50 mins**

Per portion
**511 Kcal**
**29g fat**
**(16.5g saturated)**

# Tasty potatoes

Serves 4  Ⓥ

**Baking potatoes** 4
**Butter** 25g (1oz)
**Tomatoes** 4, finely chopped
**Spring onions** 6, trimmed and sliced
**Cheddar cheese** 175g (6oz), grated

**Double Gloucester cheese** 50g (2oz), grated
**Eggs** 2, beaten
**Green salad** to serve (optional)

1   Preheat the oven to 200°C/400°F/Gas 6. Prick the potatoes with a fork and cook in the microwave for 5 minutes. Then bake in the oven for 30–40 minutes.

2   Melt the butter in a small saucepan, add half of the tomatoes and onions and cook for 5 minutes until softened, stirring, until most of the liquid has evaporated.

3   Mix the cheese and eggs together, add to the pan and stir continuously over a low heat until thickened.

4   Make a cross cut in each potato, spoon in the cheese mixture then top with the reserved tomatoes and onions. Serve with a green salad, if using.

Scan with Smartphone
for shopping list

Time required
1½–1¾ hrs

Per portion
245 Kcal
12g fat
(4.7g saturated)

# Twice-baked potatoes

Serves 4 Ⓥ

**Baking potatoes** 2 large

**Olive oil** 1 tsp

**Mature Cheddar cheese** 50–75g
(2–3oz), grated

**Milk** 1–2 tbsp

**Snipped chives** 3 tbsp

**Eggs** 4

**Baked beans** to serve (optional)

1   Preheat the oven to 220°C/425°F/Gas 7. Prick the potatoes with a fork and then brush each one lightly all over with the olive oil.

2   Place the potatoes on a baking tray and bake in the oven for 45 minutes–I hour, or until they feel soft in the centre.

3   When cooked, remove the potatoes from the oven and put them onto a board (leaving the oven on). Cut each potato in half lengthways and scoop the soft potato into a bowl, taking care to keep the skins intact. Set the skins aside.

4   Mash the cooked potato well, and then beat in the grated cheese and milk. Add the chives.

5   Spoon the potato mixture back into the potato-skins. Using the back of a spoon, make a large, deep hollow in the centre of each potato, deep enough to take an egg.

6   Place the filled potato shells on a baking tray and break the eggs into the centre of each potato. Return the potatoes to the oven and cook for 10–15 minutes, until the potato borders are golden brown and the egg whites are set, but the yolks are still soft, taking care not to overcook them. Serve at once with baked beans, if using.

**Cook's tip** For a finishing touch, sprinkle over some paprika before serving.

Time required
1 hr

Per portion
474 Kcal
42g fat
(20.1g saturated)

# Spinach & cheese roulade

Serves 4-6 Ⓥ Ⓕ

**Butter** 25g (1oz), melted

**Spinach** 275g (10oz), fresh or frozen, rinsed

**Eggs** 3, separated

**Full fat soft cheese** 275g (10oz)

**Salt and freshly ground black pepper**

**Plain yogurt** 2 tbsp

**Spring onions** 4, trimmed and sliced

**Walnuts** 50g (2oz), roughly chopped

**Double Gloucester cheese** 75g (3oz), grated

**Cayenne pepper** ½ tsp

1   Preheat the oven to 190°C/375°F/Gas 5 and line a 30 x 23cm (12 x 9in) Swiss roll tin with greaseproof paper. Brush with butter. Cook the spinach in a saucepan for 4–5 minutes until tender. Drain well and press out as much liquid as possible. Beat in the egg yolks and 75g (3oz) of the soft cheese. Season to taste.

2   In a separate bowl, whisk the egg whites with an electric hand whisk until they form stiff peaks. Fold them into the egg yolks and cheese mixture with a metal spoon. Turn the mixture into the prepared tin, smooth over and bake for 15 minutes until firm to the touch.

3   Turn out onto greaseproof paper. Cool slightly, then peel off the baking paper, trim off the outside edges and roll up with the greaseproof paper and leave to cool.

4   Mix all the remaining ingredients together in a bowl. Unroll the roulade and remove the paper. Spread with the filling and roll up once more. Serve chilled and cut into slices.

59

Time required
20 mins

Per portion
344 Kcal
18.3g fat
(3.4g saturated)

# Huevos rancheros

Serves 4 **V**

**Olive oil** 1–2 tbsp

**Onion** 1, peeled and finely chopped

**Red pepper** 1, deseeded and chopped

**Garlic** 1 clove, peeled and finely chopped

**Dried chilli flakes** generous pinch

**Thyme** small bunch, leaves plucked

**Chopped tomatoes** 400g can

**Salt and freshly ground black pepper**

**Sunflower oil** 2 tbsp

**Eggs** 4

**Tortillas** 4, warmed according to packet instructions

1   Heat the olive oil in a non-stick frying pan and add the onion, pepper and garlic. Cook for about 5 minutes or until the onions are softened but not coloured. Then add the chilli flakes, most of the thyme leaves and tomatoes together with 100ml (3½ fl oz) of water. Mix well and cook for a 5–7 minutes or until thickened and reduced. Season with salt.

2   Heat the sunflower oil in a large non-stick frying pan. Crack the eggs into the pan and fry until the whites are set but the yolks are still runny. Season with salt and pepper.

3   Pop the warm tortillas onto serving plates, add a generous spoonful of cooked tomato sauce, top with a fried egg, garnish with the remaining thyme leaves and  black pepper and serve.

**Cook's tip** To make a healthier version, use poached eggs (see page 6) instead of fried eggs.

Scan with Smartphone
for shopping list

Time required
**1 hr 20 mins**

Per portion
**456 Kcal**
**30.6g fat**
**(17.6g saturated)**

# Broccoli & courgette quiche

Serves 6 **V** **F**

### For the shortcrust pastry
**Plain flour** 225g (8oz)
**Salt** ¼ tsp
**Butter** 110g (4oz)
**Cold water** about 3 tbsp

### For the filling
**Broccoli** 150g (5oz), cut into small florets

**Courgette** 150g (5oz), diced
**Double Gloucester cheese** 110g (4oz), grated
**Eggs** 3
**Single cream** 142ml pot
**Milk** 150ml (¼ pint)
**Freshly ground black pepper**

1   Preheat the oven to 200°C/400°F/Gas 6. To make the pastry, sift the flour and salt into a bowl and add the butter. Cut into the flour with a knife, then rub it in with your fingertips until the mixture looks like fine breadcrumbs. Sprinkle some of the water over the crumbs and mix to a stiff crumbly-looking paste with a round-ended knife, adding more water if necessary. To use a food processor, see step 2 of the Quiche Lorraine on page 9.

2   Draw the pastry together with your fingertips and then turn out onto a lightly floured work surface. Knead quickly until smooth and crack-free and then roll it out to line a 20cm (8in) diameter flan tin. Prick the base then line it with greaseproof paper, add baking beans and bake for 10 minutes. Remove from the oven, lift out the paper and beans and set the case aside. Keep the oven on.

3   For the filling, cook the broccoli florets in boiling water for 2 minutes. Add the courgette and cook for 1 minute, then drain well and place in the base of the flan case with the cheese.

4   Beat the eggs, cream and milk together, season with salt and pepper and pour into the flan case. Bake for a further 35 minutes or until set. The quiche will remain a little wobbly when hot. Serve hot or cold with salad and new potatoes.

Scan with Smartphone for shopping list

# Fish

Time required
**20 mins**

Per portion
**243 Kcal
9g fat
(1.9g saturated)**

# Niçoise salad

Serves 3

**Fine green beans** 75g (3oz), trimmed

**Baby new potatoes** 150g (5oz), scrubbed

**Plum tomatoes** 2, sliced or quartered

**Red onion** 1 small, peeled and thinly sliced

**Canned artichoke hearts** 175g (6oz), drained and quartered

**Pitted black olives** 8

**Anchovy fillets in olive oil** 100g can, drained and cut in half lengthways

**Tuna in spring water** 200g can, drained

**Romaine lettuce leaves** 2–4, coarsely shredded

**Eggs** 2, hard-boiled (see page 6) and shelled

**Toasted wholemeal bread** to serve (optional)

For the dressing

**French mustard** ½ tsp

**Seasoned rice vinegar** 2 tsp

**Shredded basil leaves** a small handful

1   Cook the beans in boiling water for 5–6 minutes, until cooked yet still slightly crisp. Pour into a colander, rinse under a cold running tap and leave to cool.

2   Cook the potatoes in boiling water for 8–10 minutes, or until cooked. Pour into a colander, rinse under a cold running tap and leave to cool.

3   Meanwhile, place the tomatoes, onion, artichoke hearts, olives, anchovy fillets, tuna and lettuce leaves in a large salad bowl. Cut the beans into short lengths and the potatoes into thick slices. Then add both to the salad bowl.

4   To make the dressing, put the mustard, vinegar and basil leaves into a small bowl and whisk together.

5   Shell and slice or quarter the hard-boiled eggs. Pour the dressing over the salad and toss gently together. Arrange the eggs on top of the salad and serve at once together with some freshly toasted slices of wholemeal bread, if using.

Scan with Smartphone for shopping list

Time required
**18 mins**

Per portion
**507 Kcal**
**41.6g fat**
**(8.9g saturated)**

# Mediterranean-style smoked mackerel salad

Serves 4

**Smoked mackerel fillets with crushed peppercorns** 230g packet

**Char-grilled peppers in olive oil** 280g jar (drained weight 170g)

**Eggs** 4, hard-boiled, shelled and quartered

**Fine green beans** 125g (4oz), trimmed, halved and blanched

**Mini pitted black olives** 50g (2oz) or to taste

**Baby plum tomatoes** 4, quartered

**Romaine lettuce heart** 1, trimmed and torn into pieces

**Olive oil** 2–4 tbsp or use the oil from the jar of peppers

**Lemon** 1, juice only

1   Break the mackerel into bite-sized pieces in a bowl, discarding the skin and any bones you find. Cut the peppers into strips and add to the mackerel with the eggs, beans, olives and tomatoes. Toss together gently; the easiest way is with your hands.

2   Divide the lettuce between four plates and arrange the mackerel mix on top. Mix together the oil and lemon juice and drizzle over the salad. Serve with warm and crusty wholegrain bread.

**Cook's tip** If you don't like peppered mackerel fillets, use ready-to-eat plain hot smoked mackerel fillets instead.

69

Time required
**15 mins**

Per portion
**410 Kcal**
**30g fat**
**(11.1g saturated)**

# Japanese omelette

Serves 2

**Light olive oil** 1 tbsp

**Red pepper** ½ small, deseeded and thinly sliced

**Spring onions** 4, rimmed and thinly sliced

**Beansprouts** 110g (4oz)

**Butter** 25g (1oz)

**Cooked king prawns** 110 (4oz), roughly chopped

**Eggs** 4, seasoned and beaten

**Japanese teriyaki sauce** 2–3 tsp

1   Heat the oil in an omelette pan, add the pepper strips and spring onions and stir-fry for 2–3 minutes, until softened. Add the beansprouts and heat through for 1 minute. Remove half of the vegetables from the pan and keep warm.

2   Add half of the butter and half of the prawns to the pan and heat until the butter is sizzling. Pour in half of the beaten eggs, stir until just starting to set, then continue to cook, lifting the omelette edges with a palette knife to allow the uncooked egg to run under.

3   Sprinkle the omelette with teriyaki sauce, carefully roll it up (with the aid of the palette knife) and turn out onto a warmed plate. Then sprinkle it with a little more teriyaki sauce, if wished, and serve at once. Repeat with the remaining mixture. Serve with a crisp green salad and some crusty bread.

Scan with Smartphone for shopping list

Time required
**20 mins**

Per portion
**486 Kcal**
**35g fat**
**(16.5g saturated)**

# Cheat's omelette Arnold Bennett

Serves 2

**Smoked haddock fillet** 200g (7oz)

**Butter** 15g (½oz), plus extra for cooking each omelette

**Eggs** 4

**Freshly ground black pepper**

**Ready-made cheese sauce** 4–5 tbsp

**Gruyère cheese** 25g (1oz), grated

**Chopped parsley** to garnish

**Steamed potatoes and asparagus spears** to serve (optional)

1   Remove the skin and any bones from the haddock and cut the flesh into small chunks. Heat the butter in a small non-stick omelette pan, add the haddock and stir-fry gently for about 3 minutes until it is just cooked. Remove from the pan and set aside.

2   For each omelette, beat 2 eggs with a little pepper. Melt a little more butter (if necessary) in the same pan and when it is foaming add the eggs. Move the omelette around the pan and cook until it is just set on the bottom but still a little runny on the top.

3   Remove the pan from the heat. Scatter with half the smoked haddock and carefully spread with half the cheese sauce. Sprinkle with half the grated Gruyère cheese. Pop under a hot grill and cook until the cheese sauce is bubbling and golden. Then slide onto a warm serving plate (you may need to loosen the omelette first with a palette knife) and keep warm while you make the other omelette.

4   Serve both of the omelettes at once, scattered with the chopped parsley and with steamed potatoes and asparagus, if using.

**Cook's tip** Use any remaining cheese sauce from the pot in another dish – add to strips of hot and crispy cooked bacon, heat through and then stir through pasta cooked with peas and broccoli.

Scan with Smartphone for shopping list

Time required
**20 mins**

Per portion
**565 Kcal**
**32g fat**
**(5.1g saturated)**

# Haddock with poached egg

Serves 2

**Ciabatta loaf** half piece, or a thick slice of any day-old bread, torn into pieces

**Olive oil** 4 tbsp

**Fine green beans** 110g (4oz), trimmed and halved

**Smoked haddock** 2 fillets, each weighing about 150g (5oz)

**Eggs** 2

**White wine or cider vinegar** 4 tsp

**Wholegrain mustard** 2 tsp

**Salt and freshly ground black pepper**

1   Preheat the grill to hot. Scatter the pieces of bread on a baking sheet and sprinkle with 2 tbsp of the oil. Use your hand to coat the bread roughly in oil. Toast under the grill for 4–5 minutes until crispy and browned. Turn the bread pieces a couple of times to prevent them from burning.

2   Meanwhile, half fill a medium-sized saucepan with boiling water. Bring the water back to the boil and add the beans. Cook them for 3 minutes in the boiling water, then remove with a slotted spoon and put into a small bowl. Add 1 tbsp of the oil to the warm beans and stir to coat them.

3   Add the fish to the pan, cover and poach gently at a simmer over a low heat for 3–5 minutes, depending on the thickness of the pieces. Take the fish out with a fish slice and put onto a piece of kitchen paper on a warmed plate.

4   Add a splash of the vinegar to the pan of water, bring back to the boil and crack the eggs into the water. Poach them for 3 minutes, or to your liking.

5   Meanwhile, skin and break the fish into large flakes and put on the plate with the ciabatta croutons and beans. Place the poached eggs on top. Whisk the rest of the vinegar and the mustard into the remaining oil, then drizzle over the whole dish. Season with a little salt and lots of pepper.

Scan with Smartphone for shopping list

Time required
**55 mins**

Per portion
**357 Kcal**
**17.3g fat**
**(4.1g saturated)**

# Smoked fish kedgeree

Serves 3

**Un-dyed smoked haddock fillet**
680g (1½lb)

**Olive oil** ½ tbsp

**Red onion** 1–2 large, peeled, halved
and cut into thick wedges

**Long grain rice** 150g (5oz)

**Turmeric** a pinch

**Smoked mackerel fillets with
crushed peppercorns** 250g (9oz)

**Eggs** 2, hard-boiled, shelled and
chopped

**Watercress** 85g (3½oz), roughly
chopped

**Lemon wedges and green salad** to
serve (optional)

1   Put the haddock into a large lidded frying pan, cutting the fish into
    two pieces to fit. Barely cover the haddock with cold water and
    bring to the boil. Turn off the heat, cover with the lid and leave the
    haddock to stand for 10–15 minutes, during which time it will cook
    through completely.

2   Drain the haddock (reserving the liquid), then remove the skin,
    flake the flesh and remove any bones. Set aside while you prepare
    the rice.

3   Heat the olive oil in the frying pan, then add the onion wedges and
    cook them gently until just beginning to soften. Stir the rice into
    the onion, add 300ml (½ pint) of the reserved liquid and turmeric
    and bring to the boil. Then reduce the heat, cover the pan and
    cook gently for 20–25 minutes, until the rice is cooked.

4   Meanwhile, flake and bone the mackerel fillets. When the rice is
    cooked, gently mix in the haddock and mackerel and heat through
    until piping hot.

5   Using a fork, gently mix both the eggs and watercress into the
    kedgeree and serve at once with lemon wedges and a green
    salad, if using.

Scan with Smartphone
for shopping list

**Cook's tip** Saffron was traditionally used to turn rice a bright yellow, but
turmeric is a cheaper alternative. It is used in many curries, too.

Time required
**30 mins**

Per portion
**463 Kcal**
**15g fat**
**(2.7g saturated)**

# Special fried rice with prawns

Serves 4

**Long grain white rice** 250g (9oz)
**Eggs** 3
**Sunflower oil** 2 tbsp
**Toasted sesame oil** 1 tbsp
**Spring onions** 6, trimmed and sliced

**Red pepper** 1 large, deseeded and chopped
**Frozen peas** 100g (3½oz)
**Cooked king prawns** 250g packet
**Dried chilli flakes** a generous pinch
**Soy sauce** to serve

1   Bring a saucepan of water to the boil. Add the rice, reduce the heat, cover and simmer for 10 minutes until the rice is cooked through.

2   Meanwhile, beat the eggs in a small bowl. Heat the sunflower oil in a wok, add the eggs and gently stir in the hot oil to scramble. Remove from the wok and set aside while cooking the vegetables.

3   Pour the sesame oil into the wok and heat, then add the spring onions and pepper and stir-fry for a minute or so. Add the peas and prawns and continue stir-frying until the peas are cooked and the prawns are hot.

4   Drain the rice and add it to the prawns and vegetables together with the chilli flakes and stir-fry to mix all the ingredients well. Add the scrambled eggs and stir together. Spoon into four warmed bowls and serve with soy sauce.

**Cook's tip** This is a great vegetarian dish if you simply leave out the prawns and add an extra egg for the scramble.

Scan with Smartphone for shopping list

Time required
**30 mins**

Per portion
**306 Kcal**
**26.3g fat**
**(12.9g saturated)**

# Egg & smoked salmon timbales

Serves 4

**Smoked salmon** 175g (6oz), cut into thin strips
**Lemon juice** 1 tbsp
**Freshly ground black pepper**

**Eggs** 3
**Double cream** 150ml (¼ pint)
**Melba toast** to serve (optional)

1   Preheat the oven to 180°C/350°F/Gas 4. Thoroughly butter four 150ml (¼ pint) ramekins and set them on a baking sheet. Put the salmon strips in a bowl, toss with the lemon juice and season with pepper. Divide between the ramekins.

2   Beat the eggs with the cream, then carefully pour into the ramekins. Bake for 20–25 minutes or until puffed and just set. Serve the timbales at once with warm Melba toast, if using.

**Cook's tip** To make Melba toast, grill 4 slices of white (or brown) bread on both sides. Trim the crusts and very carefully cut each slice of toast in half horizontally. Cut the bread in half diagonally and pop back under the grill until toasted and crisp. Watch the toast as this doesn't take very long!

Time required
**55 mins**

Per portion
**347 Kcal**
**25.9g fat**
**(11.9g saturated)**

# Salmon fish cakes with rich tartare sauce

Serves 4 **F**

**Red salmon** 213g can, drained, any bones and skin removed

**Cold mashed potato** 300g (11oz) without the addition of butter or milk

**Chopped dill** 2 tbsp

**Lime** 1, grated zest and juice

**Anchovy paste** ½ tsp or to taste

**Worcestershire sauce** a dash

**Tabasco sauce** a dash

**Egg yolk** 1

**Olive oil** to drizzle

**Capers** 1–2 tbsp, drained and finely chopped

**Spring onions** 3, trimmed and finely chopped

**Chopped coriander** 2 tbsp

**Hard-boiled eggs** 2, shelled and finely chopped

**Crème fraîche** 150ml (¼ pint)

**Salt and freshly ground black pepper**

**Lemon wedges and salad** to serve (optional)

1   Preheat the oven to 190°C/375°F/Gas 5 and lightly oil a roasting tin. In a large bowl, mix together the salmon, mashed potato, dill and lime zest and juice. Season with the anchovy paste, Worcestershire sauce and Tabasco. Add the egg yolk to bind the mix together.

2   Using your hands, dipped in a little flour to stop the mix from sticking, shape into four fish cakes. Place them in the prepared roasting tin, drizzle the top of the cakes with a little oil and cook in the oven for 25–30 minutes or until starting to turn golden and piping hot.

3   Mix together the capers, spring onions, coriander and hard-boiled eggs, then stir in the crème fraîche. Season to taste. Serve the sauce with the fish cakes and lemon wedges and salad, if using.

**Cook's tip** If you prefer tuna fish cakes, simply substitute the salmon with a 175g (6oz) can of tuna in brine that has been drained. For a lower calorie tartare sauce, substitute the crème fraîche with light mayonnaise.

Scan with Smartphone for shopping list

# Meat

Time required
**30 mins**

Per portion
**471 Kcal**
**24.6g fat**
**(5g saturated)**

# Caesar salad with chicken

Serves 4

**Olive oil** 6–7 tbsp

**Skinless chicken breasts** 4, cut in half horizontally

**White bread** 4 slices, crusts removed and remaining bread cubed

**Eggs** 2 medium

**Garlic** 1 large clove

**Lemon juice** 2 tbsp from 1 lemon

**Worcestershire sauce** to taste

**Parmesan cheese** 25g (1oz), grated, plus extra to serve

**Anchovy fillets** 50g can, drained

**Romaine lettuce hearts** 2 large, trimmed and torn into pieces

**Freshly ground black pepper**

1   Heat 1 tbsp of the oil in a large non-stick saucepan until hot. Add the chicken and cook for 5–6 minutes on each side, or until cooked through. Remove from the heat and set aside.

2   Heat 2–3 tbsp of the oil in a frying pan and cook the cubes of bread until crispy and golden, stirring frequently. Remove from the pan with a slotted spoon and leave to drain on kitchen paper.

3   Tip the eggs into a pan of cold water and bring to the boil. Boil for 1 minute, then drain and plunge immediately into cold water to stop the eggs from overcooking.

4   Leave the eggs to cool in the water for a couple of minutes, then crack the eggs into a food processor with the garlic, lemon juice, Worcestershire sauce, Parmesan cheese and most of the anchovy fillets. Blend well and gradually add the remaining olive oil with the motor still running. Cut the remaining anchovies into very thin strips to garnish.

5   Arrange the lettuce in four serving bowls. Cut the chicken into strips and add to the bowls with the crispy croutons. Drizzle over the dressing and scatter with the sliced anchovies and Parmesan cheese. Add a generous grinding of black pepper and serve at once.

**Cook's tip** To serve this as a traditional starter, leave out the chicken.

Scan with Smartphone for shopping list

Time required
**40 mins**

Per portion
**504 Kcal**
**26.7g fat**
**(5.7g saturated)**

# Chicken & red pepper foo young

Serves 2

**For the sauce**

**Skinless chicken breasts** 2

**Spring onions** 6, trimmed and sliced

**Red chilli** ½, deseeded

**Root ginger** 2.5cm (1in) piece

**Soy sauce** 1 tbsp

**Caster sugar** 1 tsp

**Cornflour** 2 tsp

**For the foo young**

**Sunflower oil** 2–3 tbsp

**Spring onions** 4, trimmed and sliced

**Red pepper** 1, deseeded and chopped

**Beansprouts** 50g (2oz)

**Eggs** 4, whisked

**Chopped coriander** 2 tbsp

1   Tip the chicken, spring onions, chilli and ginger into a small saucepan with about 300ml (½ pint) of water (enough to cover the chicken) and bring to the boil. Cover, reduce the heat and simmer for 15–20 minutes or until the chicken is cooked through. Remove the chicken from the pan with a slotted spoon and set aside.

2   Strain the stock into a jug, discarding the spring onions, ginger and chilli. Tip the stock back into the pan and add the soy sauce and sugar. Mix the cornflour with a little cold water to make a paste, then add some of the hot stock and whisk this mix into the pan. Bring back to the boil, still whisking, and continue cooking until thickened. Simmer for a minute or so, continuing to whisk.

3   For the foo young, heat half the oil in a non-stick frying pan, add the spring onions, red pepper and beansprouts and stir-fry until tender. Remove from the heat and keep the vegetables warm.

4   Tip half of the eggs into the frying pan and swirl around to make an omelette. When the bottom is set, turn over with a spatula to cook the top side. Tip onto a plate and keep warm. Cook the second omelette in the same way.

5   Shred the chicken and scatter over the omelettes with the vegetables. Serve at once with the sauce and a scattering of coriander.

Scan with Smartphone for shopping list

Time required
35–45 mins

Per portion
705 Kcal
38.3g fat
(17.4g saturated)

# Chicken, broccoli & cheese pancake bake

Serves 4

**Ready-made cheese sauce** 2 x 350g pots

**Cooked skinless and boneless chicken** 300g (11oz), cut into bite-sized pieces

**Broccoli florets** 150g (5oz), cooked and drained

**Eggs** 2, hard-boiled, shelled and chopped

**Snipped chives** 2 tbsp

**Pancakes** 1 packet of 6 plain (see tip, below)

**Cheddar cheese** 25g (1oz), grated, for sprinkling

1   Preheat the oven to 200°C/400°F/Gas 6. Tip one of the pots of cheese sauce into a bowl and stir in the cooked chicken, broccoli, eggs and chives.

2   Spread some of the chicken mix down the centre of each pancake and roll up. Lay them in a lasagne dish with the seam side up and spread the remaining cheese sauce on top together with the grated Cheddar cheese.

3   Bake in the oven for 25–35 minutes or until the sauce is bubbling and the chicken mix is hot all the way through. Serve at once.

**Cook's tip** If you would rather make your own pancakes see page 7. They do taste much better!

Time required
**1 hr**

Per portion
**560 Kcal**
**38g fat**
**(20g saturated)**

# Cheddar & ham soufflé

Serves 3

**Fresh breadcrumbs** 25g (1oz)
**Butter** 25g (1oz)
**Plain flour** 25g (1oz)
**Milk** 150ml (¼ pint)
**Salt and freshly ground black pepper**
**Sweet or hot paprika** ½ tsp
**Eggs** 4, separated

**Cheddar cheese** 110g (4oz) grated, plus extra for sprinkling
**Parmesan cheese** 25g (1oz) grated, plus extra for sprinkling
**Snipped chives** 3 tbsp
**Ham** 150g (5oz), cut into thin strips

1   Preheat the oven to 190°C/375°F/ Gas 5. Grease a 750–900ml (1¼–1½ pint) soufflé dish, and sprinkle the breadcrumbs over the base and sides.

2   Melt the butter in a saucepan, add the flour, then the milk and bring up to the boil, stirring constantly. Season to taste and add the paprika. Remove the pan from the heat and allow the sauce to cool a little, then beat in the egg yolks. Add the cheeses, chives and ham.

3   Whisk the egg whites with an electric hand whisk until they form stiff peaks, then fold them into the sauce with a metal spoon. Pour the soufflé mixture into the prepared dish and sprinkle the extra cheeses over the top.

4   Place the dish on a baking tray and bake for 35–45 minutes, until the soufflé is well-risen, golden brown, and feels very firm, yet springy. Serve at once in case the soufflé collapses.

Time required
**17 mins**

Per portion
**654 Kcal**
**30g fat**
**(13.5g saturated)**

# Ham carbonara

Serves 4

**Spaghetti** 350g (12oz)

**Olive oil** 2 tbsp

**Garlic** 2 cloves, peeled and finely chopped

**Cooked ham** 250g (9oz), cut into strips

**Single cream** 300ml (½ pint)

**Eggs** 2

**Parmesan cheese** 50g (2oz), grated

**Freshly ground black pepper**

1   Cook the spaghetti in a saucepan of boiling water according to the packet's instructions.

2   Meanwhile, heat the oil in a large frying pan and cook the garlic with the ham for 5 minutes, stirring occasionally. Mix together the single cream with the eggs and most of the Parmesan cheese.

3   Drain the pasta and immediately tip it back into the pan. Stir the cream mixture and ham into the pasta and quickly mix well so that the egg doesn't curdle. Serve at once in warmed pasta bowls. Garnish with pepper and the remaining Parmesan cheese.

**Cook's tip** For a really speedy dish, buy fresh spaghetti, which cooks quickly. Dinner will be ready in just 5 minutes!

Time required
**30 mins, plus
resting**

Per portion
**448 Kcal
19.8g fat
(8g saturated)**

# Spinach, prosciutto & egg pizza

Serves 2 **F**

**Pizza base mix** 145g packet
**Hand-hot water** 100ml (3½ fl oz) or the amount it says on the packet
**Tomato pizza topping** about 3 tbsp
**Tomato** 1 small, sliced

**Baby spinach leaves** 25g (1oz), shredded
**Prosciutto** 3 thin slices, cut into strips
**Eggs** 2 small or medium
**Mozzarella cheese** 75g (drained weight), sliced

1   Preheat the oven to 220°C/425°F/Gas 7 and grease and flour a baking sheet. Make the pizza base using the water and following the packet's instructions. Roll the pizza dough into a 20cm (8in) round and place on the prepared baking sheet. Leave to prove according to the packet's instructions.

2   Spread the pizza topping over the pizza base to within 5mm of the rim. Arrange the sliced tomato just in from the edge then bake for 10 minutes.

3   Remove the pizza from the oven and scatter it with the shredded spinach leaves. Use the prosciutto strips to make circles on top of the pizza, allowing two curls on each for holding the eggs in place in the centre of the pizza. Carefully crack the eggs into the two circles made by the prosciutto and scatter the rest of the pizza with slices of mozzarella.

4   Bake in the oven for a further 5–8 minutes or until the eggs are cooked according to taste and the crust is golden. Serve at once.

**Cook's tip** You can use Serrano or Parma ham instead of prosciutto.

Scan with Smartphone for shopping list

Time required
**50 mins, plus
chilling**

Per portion
**579 Kcal
38.1g fat
(20.5g saturated)**

# Parma ham & egg quiches

Serves 4  **F**

For the shortcrust pastry

**Plain flour** 225g (8oz)

**Salt** ¼ tsp salt

**Butter** 110g (4oz)

**Cold water** about 3 tbsp

For the filling

**Parma ham** 50g (2oz), trimmed of excess fat and chopped

**Mature Cheddar cheese** 25g (1oz), grated

**Double cream** 2 tbsp

**Eggs** 4 medium, plus 1 medium egg yolk

**Freshly ground black pepper**

**Snipped chives** to garnish, optional

**New potatoes and rocket leaves** to serve (optional)

1   Preheat the oven to 190°C/375°F/Gas 5. To make the pastry, sift the flour and salt into a bowl and add the butter. Cut into the butter with a knife, then rub it in with your fingertips until the mixture looks like fine breadcrumbs. Sprinkle some of the water over the crumbs and mix to a stiff crumbly-looking paste with a round-ended knife, adding more water if necessary. To use a food processor, see step 2 of the quiche Lorraine on page 9.

2   Draw the pastry together with your fingertips and then turn out onto a lightly floured work surface. Knead quickly until smooth and crack-free. Roll out the pastry and use it to line four non-stick 10cm (4in) diameter fluted flan tins. Prick the bases and chill for 10 minutes. Line with scrunched foil and set on a baking sheet. Bake for 8–10 minutes, then remove the foil and bake for 5 minutes.

3   Fill the cases with the chopped ham and grated cheese. Beat together the cream and egg yolk, season with pepper and spoon into the pastry cases.

4   Make a slight well in the centre of each quiche and crack an egg into each one. Return to the oven for a further 10–15 minutes or until the eggs are cooked. Check after 10 minutes and then every minute or so to check. Serve hot scattered with chives and with boiled new potatoes and rocket leaves, if using.

Scan with Smartphone for shopping list

Time required
**20 mins**

Per portion
**289 Kcal**
**18g fat**
**(4.8g saturated)**

# Eggs Florentine

Serves 2

**White wine vinegar** 1 tbsp

**Eggs** 2-4

**Baby spinach leaves** 225g pack

**Leek** 1 large, trimmed, washed, halved and finely shredded

**Smoked back bacon** 4 rashers

**Low-fat plain fromage frais** 4 tbsp

**Ground nutmeg** 1¼ tsp

**Salt and freshly ground black pepper**

**Toasted wholemeal bread** buttered, to serve (optional)

1 Half fill a saucepan with water and add the vinegar. Bring the water to the boil, then reduce to a gentle simmer. Carefully break each egg into a cup and slide into the water. Simmer for 3–5 minutes. Remove from the heat and keep warm in the water until ready to serve.

2 Meanwhile, rinse the spinach and pack into a saucepan without drying. Add the leek and mix together well. Cover and place over a medium heat for 4–5 minutes until wilted.

3 Preheat the grill to hot and grill the bacon rashers until cooked, turning once. Cut into slices.

4 Meanwhile, drain the spinach and leek by pressing the vegetables against the side of a colander or sieve to remove as much liquid as possible, and return to the saucepan. Stir in the fromage frais and nutmeg and add seasoning to taste.

5 Divide the spinach between two warmed plates and top with the bacon. Drain the eggs using a slotted spoon and place one or two on top of each pile. Dust with extra nutmeg and black pepper and serve with slices of hot buttered toast, if liked.

**Cook's tip** Spinach might look bulky when it's fresh, but it wilts and reduces in size very quickly when cooked. Its flavour is intense, which is why some fromage frais stirred into the cooked spinach works so well.

Scan with Smartphone for shopping list

Time required
**1 hr 5 mins**

Per portion
**514 Kcal**
**35g fat**
**(18g saturated)**

# Leek & bacon quiche

Serves 6 **F**

### For the shortcrust pastry
**Plain flour** 225g (8oz)
**Salt** ¼ tsp salt
**Butter** 110g (4oz)
**Cold water** about 3 tbsp

### For the filling
**Smoked streaky bacon** 225g (8oz), chopped
**Leeks** 4, trimmed, washed, sliced and quartered
**Caerphilly cheese** 110g (4oz), crumbled
**Eggs** 3
**Milk** 225ml (8fl oz)
**Freshly ground black pepper**

1   Preheat the oven to 200°C/400°F/Gas 6. To make the pastry, sift the flour and salt into a bowl and add the butter. Cut into the butter with a knife, then rub it in with your fingertips until the mixture looks like fine breadcrumbs. Sprinkle some of the water over the crumbs and mix to a stiff crumbly-looking paste with a round-ended knife, adding more water if necessary. To use a food processor, see step 2 of the quiche Lorraine on page 9.

2   Draw the pastry together with your fingertips and then turn out onto a lightly floured work surface. Knead quickly until smooth and crack-free and then roll it out to line a 30 x 20cm (12 x 8in) flan tin.

3   Prick the base and then line it with greaseproof paper, add baking beans or coins and bake for 10 minutes. Remove from the oven, lift out the paper and beans and set the case aside. Reduce the oven to 180°C/350°F/Gas 4.

4   While the case is baking, cook the bacon in a frying pan until browned, then remove and add the leeks. Cook until soft. Place the bacon, leeks and cheese in the flan case.

Scan with Smartphone
for shopping list

5   Beat together the eggs and milk, season with pepper and pour into the flan. Bake for about 25 minutes until set. Cut into squares and serve either hot or cold.

Time required
**30 mins**

Per portion
**415 Kcal**
**22.4g fat**
**(9.9g saturated)**

# Potato cakes with bacon & poached egg

Serves 2

**Cold mashed potato** 300g (11oz)

**Young spinach leaves** 100g (3½oz), cooked and drained according to the packet's instructions

**Parmesan cheese** 25g (1oz), finely grated

**Snipped chives** 2 tbsp

**Back bacon** 4 rashers, de-rinded

**Tomatoes** 3 small, halved

**Eggs** 2

1  Preheat the oven to 200°C/400°F/Gas 6. Put the mashed potato into a bowl. Chop the spinach and add to the mash with the Parmesan cheese and chives then shape into four round potato cakes. Set on a non-stick baking sheet and cook for 15–20 minutes until hot and starting to become crisp around the edges.

2  Meanwhile, cook the bacon on both sides on a hot griddle (or under the grill) until crispy and cooked through. Grill or griddle the tomato halves.

3  Poach the eggs (see page 6) according to taste.

4  Place the potato cakes on two warmed plates. Top one cake with a poached egg and serve at once with the griddled tomatoes and pieces of bacon.

**Cook's tip** If you want a lower calorie version, leave out the cheese. If you don't have any Parmesan to hand, then use mature Cheddar instead.

Time required
**1 hr 10 mins,
plus chilling**

Per portion
**415 Kcal
24.9g fat
(9.4g saturated)**

# Mini pork & bacon pies

Serves 6

**Plain flour** 250g (9oz)

**Salt and freshly ground black pepper**

**White vegetable fat or lard** 50g (2oz)

**Butter** 50g (2oz)

**Onion** 1 small, peeled and halved

**Boneless pork loin steaks** 175g (6oz), cut into thick strips

**Unsmoked back bacon** 3 rashers, de-rinded and cut into thick strips

**Chopped sage** 1 tbsp

**Chopped parsley** 1–2 tbsp

**Eggs** 3 medium, hard-boiled, shelled and cut in half

**Egg yolk** 1, beaten

**Powdered gelatine** ½ tsp

**Boiling ham stock** (from a stock cube) 50ml (2fl oz)

**Pickled onions and celery** to serve (optional)

1   Preheat the oven to 190°C/375°F/Gas 5. Sift the flour into a bowl and season with salt. Melt the fat and butter in a pan with 125ml (4fl oz) of water. Bring to the boil, then pour the liquid into the flour, continuously stirring. Press the mixture into a smooth ball using the back of a spoon. Cover the bowl and set aside.

2   Tip the onion into a food processor and blend until finely chopped. Add the pork and bacon and pulse to chop the meat finely. Add the herbs and plenty of black pepper and pulse again.

3   Knead the pastry on a floured work surface, then roll out to 3mm (⅛in) thickness. With a 13cm (5in) and a 7.5cm (3in) plain round cutter, stamp out six cases and six lids. Line a six-hole deep muffin tin with the cases, ensuring the pastry overlaps the top of the holes. Divide half the meat between the cases. Add half an egg to each and top with the remaining meat. Dampen the rims with egg yolk and press the lids in place. Pinch the edges to seal. Brush the tops with egg yolk, make a small slit in the top of each pie and bake for 40 minutes or until golden. Leave to cool for about 15 minutes then remove to a wire rack.

4   Dissolve the gelatine in the ham stock according to the packet's instructions. Open the slit in the top of each pie with a knife then use a teaspoon to pour gelatine into each slit. Chill for up to 24 hours before serving.

Scan with Smartphone for shopping list

Time required
**1hr, plus standing**

Per portion
**605 Kcal**
**37.4g fat**
**(12.3g saturated)**

# Toad in the hole with onion gravy

Serves 4

**Plain flour** 110g (4oz), plus about 25g (1oz) for the onion gravy

**Eggs** 3

**Milk** 150ml (¼ pint)

**Sunflower oil** 2 tbsp

**Pork sausages** 8

**Butter** 25g (1oz)

**Onions** 3, halved, peeled and finely sliced

**Soft light brown sugar** 1 tsp

**Beef stock** 600ml (1 pint)

**Salt and freshly ground black pepper**

1   Preheat the oven to 220°C/425°F/Gas 7. For the batter, sift the flour into a bowl, make a well in the centre and gradually whisk in the eggs, followed by the milk and 150ml (¼ pint) of water. Continue whisking until you have a smooth batter and then leave to stand.

2   Put 1 tbsp of the oil into a roasting tin and add the sausages. Cook in the oven for 10 minutes or until the oil is sizzling hot and the sausages are starting to brown. Remove from the oven, pour the batter around the sausages, and cook for 30–40 minutes or until puffed and golden.

3   Meanwhile, make the gravy in a large heavy-based pan. Melt the butter and remaining oil over a medium heat until the butter is foaming. Add the onions and cook for about 10 minutes, stirring occasionally. Add the sugar, inrease the heat and cook for a further 5–10 minutes, stirring occasionally, until the onions are golden. Remove from the heat, add the flour and mix well (the amount of flour you use depends on how thick you like your gravy). Gradually add the stock and mix until the gravy is smooth.

4   Return the pan to the heat and bring slowly to the boil, stirring all the time, then simmer for a couple of minutes. Season to taste. Divide the toad in the hole onto four warmed plates and serve with the onion gravy and steamed green vegetables such as broccoli or peas.

Scan with Smartphone for shopping list

Time required
**40 minutes**

Per portion
425 Kcal
28.6g fat
(10.5g saturated)

# Eggs Andalusia

Serves 4

**Olive oil** 3 tbsp
**New potatoes** 250g (9oz), diced
**Onion** 1 large, peeled and diced
**Garlic** 1 clove, peeled and crushed
**Red pepper** 1, deseeded and diced
**Fine green beans** 200g (7oz), cut into 2.5cm (1in) lengths
**Frozen peas** 200g (7oz)

**Salt and freshly ground black pepper**
**Eggs** 4
**Chorizo sausages** 2 x 10cm (4in), sliced at an angle
**Chopped parsley** 1 tbsp
**Cheddar cheese** 25g (1oz), grated, for sprinkling

1 Preheat the oven to 180°C/350°F/Gas 4. Heat 2 tbsp of the oil in a frying pan until hot. Add the diced potatoes and fry until crisp. Remove to a plate with a slotted spoon and set aside.

2 Add the remaining oil to the pan and cook the onion, garlic and pepper for 5 minutes.

3 Lightly steam the beans and peas for about 5 minutes, until just tender. Add to the onion and pepper. Fry for a further 5 minutes, then gently stir in the potatoes. Season to taste.

4 Pour the vegetables into a large ovenproof dish and make four hollows on the surface. Break an egg into each hollow.

5 Arrange the chorizo slices around the eggs and sprinkle with the parsley and cheese. Bake for 10–15 minutes, until the egg whites are just set.

111

Time required
**45 mins**

Per portion
**636 Kcal**
**22.1g fat**
**(10.2g saturated)**

# Chilli beef pancakes

Serves 4 **F**

**Minced beef** 250g (9oz)

**Onion** 1, peeled and chopped

**Garlic** 1 clove, peeled and crushed

**Red kidney beans** 400g can, rinsed and drained

**Baked beans** 415g can

**Chopped tomatoes** 400g can

**Yellow pepper** 1, deseeded and chopped

**Chilli powder** 1 tsp

**Pancakes** 8, freshly cooked (see page 7)

**Red Leicester cheese** 50g (2oz), grated

**Salad** to serve (optional)

1   Heat a saucepan over a medium heat, add the beef and onion and dry fry for 5 minutes until the beef has browned. Add the garlic, kidney beans, baked beans, tomatoes, pepper and chilli powder and mix together well. Cover and simmer for 30 minutes, topping up with a little water if the mixture begins to stick.

2   Heat the grill to hot. Divide the filling between the pancakes and fold into triangles, then place in a baking dish in one layer. Sprinkle with the cheese and grill until it has melted. Serve on warmed plates with some salad, if using.

113

# Bakes

Time required
**30 mins**

Per scone
**148 Kcal**
**7.3g fat**
**(4.3g saturated)**

# Lancashire cheese scones

Serves 12 **V** **F**

**Self-raising flour** 250g (9oz)
**Baking powder** 1 tsp
**Mustard powder** ½ tsp
**Butter** 50g (2oz), plus extra to serve (optional)

**Lancashire cheese** 110g (4oz), grated
**Egg** 1
**Milk** 125ml (4fl oz), plus extra for glaze

1  Preheat the oven to 220°C/425°F/Gas 7 and butter a baking sheet. Sift the flour, baking powder and mustard into a bowl. Add the butter and then rub it in until the mixture resembles fine breadcrumbs. Stir in 75g (3oz) of the cheese.

2  Lightly beat the egg into the milk and then pour into the flour mixture. Use a round-ended knife to bind together the ingredients. Turn out onto a lightly floured work surface and knead very gently for less than 20 seconds.

3  Roll out the dough very gently (see tip on page 119) to a 2cm (¾in) thickness and cut out rounds using a 6.5cm (2½in) plain cutter, re-rolling as necessary. Transfer the scones to the prepared baking sheet.

4  Brush the tops of the scones with a little milk and then sprinkle over the remaining grated cheese. Bake the scones towards the top of the oven for 12–15 minutes until they have risen and are a light golden colour. Remove from the oven, transfer to a wire rack and leave to cool. Serve them warm or cold and with some butter, if using.

**Cook's tip** The Lancashire cheese gives a delicate flavour to these scones. If you prefer a stronger cheese flavour, then use an equal quantity of a mature Cheddar cheese.

Scan with Smartphone
for shopping list

Time required
**25 mins**

Per scone
**223 Kcal**
**8.5g fat**
**(4.3g saturated)**

# Chilli & oatmeal scones

Makes 16 **V** **F**

**Self-raising flour** 500g (1lb 2oz)

**Fine oatmeal** 150g (5oz), plus extra for sprinkling (optional)

**Baking powder** 2 tsp

**Salt** a pinch

**Butter** 110g (4oz), plus extra to serve (optional)

**Caster sugar** 2 tbsp

**Dried chilli flakes** 1 tsp

**Eggs** 2, plus 1 beaten to glaze

**Milk** 300ml (½ pint)

1   Preheat the oven to 220°C/425°F/Gas 7 and butter a baking sheet. Mix together the flour, oatmeal, baking powder and salt in a bowl. Then rub in the butter until the mixture resembles fine crumbs. Stir in the sugar and chilli flakes.

2   Lightly beat two eggs into the milk and then pour into the flour mixture. Use a round-ended knife to bind together the ingredients. Turn out onto a lightly floured work surface and knead very gently for less than 20 seconds.

3   Divide the dough into two. Roll out one portion at a time very gently (see Tip, below) to a 2cm (¾in) thickness and, using a 7cm (2¾in) plain round cutter, stamp out eight rounds, re-rolling as necessary. Transfer the scones to the prepared baking sheet. Repeat with the second portion of dough.

4   Carefully use the beaten egg to glaze just the top of the scones (if the glaze goes down the sides it will prevent them from rising) and spinkle over the extra oatmeal, if using. Bake the scones towards the top of the oven for 12–15 minutes until they have risen and are a light golden colour. Remove from the oven, transfer to a wire rack and leave to cool. Serve them warm or cold and with some butter, if using.

Scan with Smartphone for shopping list

**Cook's tip** Often, the reason scones don't rise is that they are rolled out too heavily, or too much. You could alternatively gently pat the scone dough into a round before cutting out the scone rounds.

Time required
**30 mins**

Per muffin
**175 Kcal**
**6.8g fat**
**(3.7g saturated)**

# Extra mature Cheddar muffins

Makes 12 **Ⓥ Ⓕ**

**Self-raising flour** 300g (11oz)
**Baking powder** 1 tsp
**Bicarbonate of soda** ½ tsp
**Caster sugar** 25g (1oz)

**Extra mature Cheddar cheese** 150g (5oz), grated
**Full-fat milk** 300ml (½ pint)
**Eggs** 2, beaten

1   Preheat the oven to 200°C/400°F/Gas 6 and line a 12-hole muffin tin with paper cases. Sift together all the dry ingredients into a bowl and lightly mix together. Then add the cheese and rub into the flour mix very gently.

2   Whisk together the milk and eggs in a jug. Gently fold the liquid into the dry ingredients, taking care not to overmix.

3   Divide the batter between the muffin cases and bake for 18–20 minutes or until well risen and golden. Serve warm or cold.

**Cook's tip** If you are a fan of blue cheese and you want a very adult muffin, try crumbling 150g (5oz) of blue cheese with 50g (2oz) chopped walnuts instead of mature Cheddar cheese.

Time required
**30 mins**

Per muffin
**274 Kcal**
**11g fat**
**(6.4g saturated)**

# Banana & cinnamon muffins

Makes 12 muffins   Ⓥ Ⓕ

**Self-raising flour** 300g (11oz)

**Baking powder** 1 tsp

**Bicarbonate of soda** ½ tsp

**Ground cinnamon** ½ tsp

**Demerara sugar** 200g (7oz)

**Full fat milk** 300ml (½ pint)

**Butter** 125g (4½oz), melted

**Eggs** 2

**Peeled bananas** 200g (7oz) (about 2), finely chopped

1 Preheat the oven to 200°C/400°F/Gas 6 and line a 12-hole muffin tin with paper cases. Sift together all the dry ingredients, except the sugar, into a bowl and lightly mix together. Then add the sugar and mix into the flour.

2 Whisk together the milk, melted butter and eggs in a jug. Stir in the chopped banana. Gently fold the liquid into the dry ingredients, taking care not to overmix.

3 Divide the batter between the muffin cases and bake for 15–20 minutes or until well risen and golden. Serve warm or cold.

**Cook's tip** If you don't have a banana to hand, try this recipe with the same weight of frozen raspberries or blueberries or even a mixture – don't let them thaw.

123

Scan with Smartphone for shopping list

Time required
1 hr 5 mins

Per square
245 Kcal
9.9g fat
(5.6g saturated)

# Cranberry bread pudding

Makes 16 squares  Ⓥ Ⓕ

**Milk** 375ml (13fl oz)

**White bread** 225g (8oz), crust removed, bread torn into small pieces

**Oranges** grated zest of 2, plus juice of 1

**Mixed ground spice** 1 tbsp

**Seedless raisins** 175g (6oz)

**Sultanas** 150g (5oz)

**Mixed chopped peel** 50g (2oz)

**Ready-to-eat prunes** 75g (3oz), chopped

**Ready-to-eat dried apricots** 75g (3oz), chopped

**Dried cranberries** 75g (3oz)

**Eggs** 3, beaten

**Butter** 150g (5oz), melted

**Black treacle** 1–2 tbsp

**Granulated sugar** 50g (2oz), plus extra for sprinkling

1  Preheat the oven to 180°C/350°F/Gas 4 and grease a 23cm (9in) square shallow baking dish. Pour the milk into a bowl, add the bread and leave to soak for 10 minutes. Add the rest of the ingredients, including the 50g (2oz) of sugar, and mix well.

2  Transfer the mixture to the prepared baking dish and spread evenly. Bake for 45–50 minutes until the pudding is lightly browned and set in the centre.

3  Sprinkle with granulated sugar and serve hot or cold, cut into chunky squares.

125

Scan with Smartphone
for shopping list

Time required
**1 hr 30 mins,
plus cooling**

Per slice
**294 Kcal
13.6g fat
(7.8g saturated)**

# Cherry cake

Makes 16 slices  Ⓥ Ⓕ

**Glacé cherries** 200g tub

**Butter** 225g (8oz), softened

**Caster sugar** 225g (8oz)

**Eggs** 4

**Lemon** 1, grated zest and juice

**Self-raising flour** 350g (12oz)

**Milk** 3 tbsp

**Chopped mixed peel** 1 tbsp

**Sugar lumps** 3, crushed

1   Preheat the oven to 160°C/325°F/Gas 3 and grease and line a 20cm (8in) deep cake tin with greaseproof paper. Rinse the cherries under warm water, dry them thoroughly in a tea towel and cut into quarters.

2   Cream together the butter and sugar until fluffy and then beat in the eggs, one at a time. Stir in the lemon zest and juice.

3   Toss the cherries in some of the flour. Fold in the rest of the flour, then stir in the cherries and milk. Spoon into the prepared tin and smooth the top, making a very slight dip in the middle. Sprinkle the mixed peel and crushed sugar lumps over the top. Bake for about 1 hour 15 minutes until the cake is golden, well risen and a skewer inserted into the centre comes out cleanly.

4   Take the cake out of the oven and leave to cool in the tin for about 15 minutes. Then turn onto a wire rack to cool before cutting into slices to serve.

**Cook's tip** The cake will keep in an airtight tin for a week.

Scan with Smartphone
for shopping list

Time required
**1 hr, plus cooling**

Per slice
**390 Kcal**
**30g fat**
**(10.6g saturated)**

# Simple Spanish almond cake with berries

Makes 10 slices **V**

**Eggs** 4, separated
**Caster sugar** 175g (6oz)
**Almond extract** 1 tsp (optional)
**Ground almonds** 200g (7oz)

For the topping

**Double cream** 300ml (½ pint), whipped
**Fresh berries** 300g punnet mixture of strawberries, blackberries and blueberries
**Cocoa powder** for dusting, sifted

1   Preheat the oven to 180°C/350°F/Gas 4 and grease and line a 20cm (8in) round, deep cake tin. Whisk the egg yolks and half of the sugar with an electric hand whisk until they are pale and thick enough to leave a ribbon-like trail when you lift out the whisk. Rinse the beaters and dry thoroughly, then whisk the egg whites with the electric hand whisk until they form stiff peaks. Continue whisking while gradually adding the remaining sugar.

2   Gently fold the almond extract (if using) and ground almonds into the egg yolk mixture. If you find the mixture is too stiff, stir in 1 tbsp warm water. Then add one-third of the egg whites and fold in to loosen the mixture. Gently fold in the remaining egg whites.

3   Spoon into the prepared tin, level the surface, and bake for 45–50 minutes or until risen and firm to the touch. (Cover the cake with a sheet of greaseproof paper if it is browning too much.) Leave to cool in the tin for 20 minutes before turning out onto a wire rack to finish cooling, then put the cake on a flat plate.

4   Spread the cream generously on top of the cake. Sprinkle liberally with berries (slice the strawberries) and dust the top of the cake with cocoa powder.

**Cook's tip** The perfect gluten-free cake! For a lower calorie option omit the cream and serve dusted with icing sugar and fresh raspberries.

Scan with Smartphone for shopping list

Time required
**1 hr 10 mins,
plus cooling**

Per slice
**417 Kcal
27.9g fat
(11g saturated)**

# Lemon polenta cake with fruit compote

Makes 12 slices  Ⓥ

**Butter** 225g (8oz), softened

**Caster sugar** 225g (8oz)

**Eggs** 3

**Lemon extract** 1 tsp

**Ground almonds** 225g (8oz)

**Polenta** (fine cornmeal) 110g (4oz)

**Baking powder** 1 tsp

**Greek yogurt** to serve (optional)

For the fruit compote

**Frozen Black Forest fruit mix** 500g packet containing dark cherries, grapes, blackberries and blackcurrants

**Cornflour** 1 tsp

**Caster sugar** 50g (2oz)

1  Preheat the oven to 170°C/325°F/Gas 3 and grease and line a 20cm (8in) round, deep cake tin. Beat the butter and sugar in a bowl until pale and light. In a separate bowl, beat the eggs with the lemon extract. Then gradually add the eggs and lemon to the butter, beating well after each addition.

2  Fold in the almonds, polenta and baking powder. Spoon the mix into the tin, level the surface with a spatula and bake for 50–60 minutes until well risen and golden. Leave to cool in the tin for 10 minutes before turning out onto a wire rack to finish cooling.

3  Meanwhile, to make the compote, put all the ingredients in a large saucepan and heat gently, stirring occasionally. Continue cooking until the berries are heated through and the juices have thickened.

4  Serve the cake cut into wedges with a spoonful of the compote and a dollop of yogurt, if using.

**Cook's tip** If you can't find lemon extract, use the grated zest of 2 lemons instead. Packets of frozen fruit are an economical way of making fruit compote.

Scan with Smartphone
for shopping list

Time required
1¼ hrs, plus
chilling

Per slice
466 Kcal
33.1g fat
(17g saturated)

# Chocolate truffle cake

Serves 12 **V** **F**

**Dark chocolate** 425g (15oz)

**Butter** 90g (3½oz)

**Caster sugar** 150g (5oz)

**Instant coffee granules** 2 tsp

**Eggs** 4, separated

**Plain flour** 40g (1½oz)

**Ground hazelnuts or almonds** 25g (1oz)

**Double cream** 300ml (½ pint)

**Cherries or strawberries** to decorate

1   Preheat the oven to 170°C/325°F/Gas 3 and grease and line a 21.5cm (8½in) cake tin. Break the chocolate into small pieces and melt 150g (5oz) in a heatproof bowl set over a saucepan of very gently simmering water, making sure the bottom of the bowl isn't touching the water. Stir frequently until the chocolate has melted. Carefully remove the bowl from the heat and leave to cool.

2   In a separate bowl, cream together the butter and sugar until pale and fluffy. Dissolve the coffee granules in 2 tbsp of hot water. Then beat the coffee into the butter mixture with the melted chocolate and egg yolks.

3   Whisk the egg whites with an electric hand whisk until they form stiff peaks, then fold them into the mixture with a metal spoon.

133

4   Fold in the flour and ground nuts and pour the mixture into the prepared cake tin. Bake in the oven for about 40 minutes until the cake is slightly cracked with a crusty top and a skewer comes out cleanly when inserted into the centre of the cake. Leave the cake to cool in the tin for 15 minutes, then turn it out onto a rack.

5   For the icing, pour the cream into a saucepan and slowly heat it until the cream is bubbling around the edges. Remove the pan from the heat and stir in the remaining broken up chocolate. Stand, covered, until the chocolate melts, mix well then chill for 30–45 minutes or until it is firm enough to hold a peak.

Scan with Smartphone for shopping list

6   Cover the top and sides of the cake with the chocolate cream and swirl. Decorate with cherries or strawberries and serve.

Time required
**30 mins**

Per cookie
**146 Kcal**
**4g fat**
**(2.3g saturated)**

# Chocolate meringue cookies

Makes 10 cookies  (V)

**Dark chocolate** 100g bar
**Egg whites** 2
**Icing sugar** 110g (4oz)

**Water biscuits** 110g (4oz), finely crushed
**Vanilla extract** a few drops

1   Preheat the oven to 180°C/350°/Gas 4 and line a baking sheet with greaseproof paper. Break the chocolate into small pieces and melt in a heatproof bowl set over a saucepan of very gently simmering water, making sure the bottom of the bowl isn't touching the water. Stir frequently until the chocolate has melted. Carefully remove the bowl from the heat and leave to cool.

2   Whisk the egg whites with an electric hand whisk until they form stiff peaks. Continue whisking while gradually adding the sugar. Then carefully fold into the biscuit crumbs, melted chocolate and vanilla with a metal spoon.

3   Place dessertspoonfuls of the mixture onto the lined baking sheet, flattening them slightly. Bake in the centre of the oven for 12–15 minutes or until firm to the touch. Leave to cool for 1 minute on the baking sheet before moving to a wire rack to finish cooling.

**Cook's tip** To crush the water biscuits, pulse them in a food processor until finely ground, or place in a plastic bag and crush with a rolling pin.

Scan with Smartphone
for shopping list

Time required
**30–40 mins,
plus cooling**

Per brownie
**223 Kcal
12.5g fat
(7.2g saturated)**

# Deep dark brownies

Makes 16  Ⓥ Ⓕ

**Dark chocolate** 200g (7oz)

**Butter** 150g (5oz), cubed

**Eggs** 3, beaten

**Cold strong coffee** 2 tbsp

**Caster sugar** 225g (8oz)

**Self-raising flour** 90g (3½oz)

1 Preheat the oven to 180°C/350°F/Gas 4 and grease and line an 18cm (7in) square tin. Break the chocolate into small pieces and melt with the butter in a heatproof bowl set over a saucepan of very gently simmering water, making sure the bottom of the bowl isn't touching the water. Stir frequently until the chocolate has melted. Carefully remove the bowl from the heat and leave to cool.

2 Lightly beat the eggs with the coffee. Stir the sugar into the melted chocolate followed by the egg mixture. Sift in the flour and gently fold together using a large metal spoon.

3 Pour into the prepared tin, spread the surface flat with a spatula and bake for 20–30 minutes. Check them after 20 minutes because if you overcook them, the brownies may be a little too dry. They are ready when they are just firm to the touch on the top but still a little bit wobbly underneath. Leave to cool in the tin, then turn out onto a chopping board. Cut into 16 chocolate brownies.

**Cook's tip** If you don't like the combination of chocolate and coffee, then add 2 tbsp of water instead of 2 tbsp strong coffee to the eggs.

Time required
**25 mins**

Per cookie
**225 Kcal**
**12.2g fat**
**(7.3g saturated)**

# Cranberry & white chocolate cookies

Makes 20 **V** **F**

**Butter** 200g (7oz), softened
**Soft light brown sugar** 150g (5oz)
**Eggs** 2, beaten

**Self-raising flour** 300g (11oz)
**White chocolate** 200g (7oz), chopped
**Dried cranberries** 75g packet

1   Preheat the oven to 190°C/375°F/Gas 5 and line a baking sheet with baking parchment. Beat the butter with the sugar in a bowl with a wooden spoon. Add the eggs and flour and mix well. Work the chopped chocolate and cranberries into the mixture.

2   Drop generous dessertspoonfuls of the mix onto the prepared baking sheet and cook in batches for 10–15 minutes until the cookies are golden, but still soft. Leave to cool for 1 minute on the baking sheet before moving to a wire rack to finish cooling.

**Cook's tip** This is one of those wonderful recipes that is great to get children interested in baking as it doesn't involve the use of an electric mixer – just keep an eye on where the white chocolate ends up!

139

Scan with Smartphone
for shopping list

# Desserts

Time **15 mins,
plus freezing**

Per portion
**382 Kcal
30g fat
(14g saturated)**

# Whisky & honey ice cream

Serves 8  **V** **F**

**Eggs** 4, separated
**Caster sugar** 75g (3oz)
**Heather honey** 2 tbsp
**Double cream** 300ml (½ pint)

**Whisky** 4 tbsp
**Oatmeal** 4 tbsp, toasted
**Raspberries** to decorate

1   Whisk the egg whites with an electric hand whisk until they form stiff peaks. Continue whisking while gradually adding the sugar and honey. The mixture should look thick and glossy, like meringue. Still continuing to whisk, add the egg yolks.

2   In a separate bowl, whip the cream until just peaking and then fold it into the egg mixture along with the whisky and oatmeal.

3   Transfer to a freezer-proof container and leave to freeze overnight. Stand at room temperature for 5–10 minutes before scooping and serving layered in tall glasses with fresh raspberries.

**Cook's tip** You will find oatmeal with baking ingredients in the supermarket. Oatmeal is ground to different textures, and medium oatmeal is good for this recipe as it gives a little texture and oaty bite to the flavour. Use fine ground for a smoother texture.

143

Scan with Smartphone
for shopping list

Time **15 mins**,
plus cooling and
freezing

Per portion
**388 Kcal**
**26.9g fat**
**(13g saturated)**

# Ginger ice cream

Serves 4 **V F**

**Milk** 300ml (½ pint)
**Double cream** 150ml (¼ pint)
**Caster sugar** 75g (3oz)

**Egg yolks** 4 medium
**Stem ginger in syrup** 50g (2oz), drained weight, plus extra, chopped, to decorate

1    Put the milk, cream and sugar into a saucepan and gently heat, stirring frequently, until the sugar has dissolved. Then bring the mixture slowly to the bowl.

2    Meanwhile, beat the egg yolks together in a bowl. Gradually pour the boiling milk mixture onto the egg yolks in a slow, steady stream, whisking all the time. Strain the custard into a metal loaf tin and leave to cool. Cover and freeze for 4–6 hours or until set.

3    Tip the stem ginger into a food processor and blitz until it forms a paste. Add a quarter of the ice cream to the processor and blitz again, then gradually add the rest of the ice cream, a spoonful at a time, with the motor still running. Taste the mixture and make sure you are happy with the amount of ginger; if you like it a little spicier, add a little more.

4    Return the ice cream back to the loaf tin, scatter over the extra stem ginger and freeze for at least 6 hours – overnight would be better – or until firm. Before serving, leave the ice cream at room temperature for 5–10 minutes. Serve in scoops on its own or with fresh berries, slices of fresh mango or the autumn fruit sauce on page 159.

**Cook's tip** Use two of the leftover egg whites to make a Pavlova (see page 153). Because homemade ice creams have no preservatives, they are best served within 48 hours of making.

Scan with Smartphone
for shopping list

Time **15 mins,
plus chilling**

Per portion
**268 Kcal
13.6g fat
(6g saturated)**

# Chocolate & Courvoisier brandy mousse

Serves 4  Ⓥ

**Dark chocolate** 110g (4oz)
**Eggs** 4 medium, separated
**Courvoisier brandy** 2 tbsp or to taste
**Caster sugar** 25g (1oz)

**Raspberries or strawberries** to decorate
**Cocoa powder** for dusting, sifted (optional)

1  Break the chocolate into small pieces and melt in a heatproof bowl set over a saucepan of very gently simmering water, making sure the bottom of the bowl isn't touching the water. Stir frequently and then carefully remove the bowl from the heat. Mix the egg yolks with the brandy and stir into the melted chocolate.

2  Whisk the egg whites with an electric hand whisk until they form stiff peaks. Continue whisking while gradually adding the sugar. Fold one-third of the egg whites into the chocolate with a metal spoon to loosen the mix, then gently fold in the remainder.

3  Spoon the chocolate mousse into four glasses. Cover and chill for at least 4 hours or until set.

4  Decorate with raspberries or strawberries and a dusting of sifted cocoa powder, if using.

**Cook's tip** If you are making this for friends or family who don't like brandy, use 2 tbsp of water instead. It will taste just as good.

Scan with Smartphone for shopping list

Time 1½ hrs, plus
cooling

Per portion
285 Kcal
9.3g fat
(3.3g saturated)

# Crème caramel

Serves 4  Ⓥ

**Caster sugar** 125g (4½oz)    **Milk** 600ml (1 pint)
**Eggs** 4    **Vanilla extract** ½ tsp

1   Preheat the oven to 170°C/325°F/Gas 3 and grease a 900ml
    (1½ pint) ovenproof dish. Put 110g (4oz) of the sugar and 150ml
    (¼ pint) of cold water into a heavy-based saucepan. Stand over a
    low heat and stir until the sugar dissolves.

2   Bring the liquor to the boil, then boil more briskly – without stirring
    – until the syrup turns a deep gold. Remove from the heat and add
    2 tbsp of boiling water (stand well back as it will spit), tilt to mix
    and pour the syrup into the prepared dish. Tilt the dish quickly so
    the base is covered with caramel.

3   Lightly whisk the eggs in a bowl. Warm the milk and pour it onto
    the eggs, and whisk in the vanilla and the remaining sugar. Strain
    into the dish and stand in a roasting tin containing enough hot
    water to come half way up the sides of the dish.

4   Bake for 1 hour or until set. Remove from the oven and leave to
    cool, preferably overnight, then turn out onto a serving dish. To
    do this, stand the dish in a bowl of boiling water for 1 minute,
    then loosen the top edge of the custard with a round-bladed
    knife. Invert the dish onto a serving plate and jerk the container to
    release the caramel. Serve chilled.

**Cook's tip** To make individual crèmes caramel, follow the recipe above, but spoon
equal amounts into greased ramekins. Leave until cold. Stand in boiling water for 5
minutes before unmoulding.

149

Time 1¼ hrs, plus
overnight and
chilling

Per portion
727 Kcal
74g fat
(39g saturated)

# Créme brûlées

Serves 6 **V**

**Egg yolks** 6
**Caster sugar** 50g (2oz)

**Double cream** 750ml (1¼ pints)
**Vanilla pods** 2 or use 1 tsp **vanilla essence**

1   Place the egg yolks in a large mixing bowl, add 25g (1oz) of the sugar and whisk with an electric hand whisk until they are pale in colour and very thick.

2   Pour the cream into a saucepan. Cut each vanilla pod lengthways (if using), remove the curd from the centre and add it to the cream, along with the outer skin. Gently heat the cream until hot, taking care not to let it boil. If using the vanilla pods, strain the cream to remove them, then whisk the cream into the egg yolks and sugar.

3   Place the bowl over a saucepan of gently boiling water and stir continuously until the mixture thickens enough to hold a light trail – do not be tempted to hurry the process (it can take up to an hour), as the mixture will curdle.

4   Pour the custard into six 150ml (¼ pint) flameproof ramekins. Place them on a large plate or small tray and allow the custards to cool. Cover with cling film and refrigerate overnight.

5   The next day, preheat the grill until very hot. Sprinkle the remaining sugar evenly over the top of each custard and put the dishes in a grill pan or on a baking tray. Place under the grill for 1–2 minutes until the sugar melts and turns to a golden caramel colour.

6   Allow the caramel to cool and harden, then cover with foil or cling film and chill for at least 4–5 hours to re-set the custard.

Scan with Smartphone for shopping list

**Cook's tip** Provided they are well covered, the brûléed custards will keep well for two days in the refrigerator. The actual making of crème brûlée is very simple – it just can't be hurried.

Time **55 mins**,
**plus cooling**

Per portion
**312 Kcal**
**20.2g fat**
**(11.3g saturated)**

# Pavlovas with strawberries & Limoncello cream topping

Serves 4 **V**

**Egg whites** 2 medium
**Caster sugar** 110g (4oz)
**Cornflour** ½ tsp
**White wine vinegar** ½ tsp

**Double cream** 150ml (¼ pint)
**Limoncello** 2 tbsp (optional)
**Strawberries** about 150g (5oz), hulled and sliced

1   Preheat the oven to 140°C/275°F/Gas 1. Line a baking sheet with a double thickness of greaseproof or non-stick baking paper and draw on four 9cm (3½in) circles.

2   Whisk the egg whites with an electric hand whisk until they form stiff peaks. Continue whisking while gradually adding the sugar. Mix the cornflour and vinegar in a tiny bowl and gently fold into the whisked egg whites. Divide the mixture into four and mound onto the marked circles.

3   Bake on the bottom shelf in the oven for 40–45 minutes or until the Pavlovas are crisp and dry. Then carefully remove from the baking parchment and leave to cool.

4   Whip the cream with the Limoncello, if using, until thick and place in the centre of each meringue base. Decorate with sliced strawberries and serve.

153

**Cook's tip** If you want to make chocolate swirl Pavlovas, put a little cocoa powder in a mini sieve and lightly dust over each meringue before putting it into the oven. Use the end of a knife or a cocktail stick to swirl the cocoa into the meringue. Don't add the lemon liqueur to the topping.

Scan with Smartphone
for shopping list

Time **50 mins**,
**plus cooling**

Per portion
**523 Kcal**
**34.2g fat**
**(17.5g saturated)**

# Classic retro trifle

Serves 6  Ⓥ

**Homemade Swiss roll** filled with raspberry jam, trimmed and cut into 8 slices (see Tip, below)

**Raspberries** 150g punnet

**Sherry** 2 tbsp

**Milk** 300ml (½ pint)

**Vanilla bean paste** 1 tsp or 1 **vanilla pod**, halved

**Caster sugar** 25g (1oz)

**Cornflour** 2 tsp

**Egg yolks** 3 medium

For the syllabub

**Double cream** 300ml (½ pint)

**Icing sugar** 25g (1oz) or to taste

**Sherry** 2 tbsp

To decorate

**Raspberries** 150g punnet

**Toasted flaked almonds**

1   Arrange the slices of Swiss roll around the sides and bottom of a trifle or glass dish. Scatter with the raspberries and then drizzle over the sherry.

2   Gently heat the milk, vanilla bean paste (or pod) and sugar in a saucepan until almost boiling. Mix together the cornflour and egg yolks in a bowl, then gradually add the hot milk, continuously whisking, in a very slow and steady stream.

3   Pour the custard back into the pan and heat it very gently until the custard has just thickened. Remove the pan from the heat and strain over the raspberries in the trifle bowl. Leave to cool.

4   For the syllabub, whisk the cream, sugar and sherry together in a bowl with an electric hand whisk until they are thick. Spoon the mixture over the trifle, swirling it with a fork to look pretty. Cover and chill for up to 4 hours. Just before serving, decorate with raspberries and toasted flaked almonds.

**Cook's tip** Make the Swiss roll using 3 medium eggs whisked with 75g (3oz) caster sugar until very pale and thick. Quickly fold in 75g (3oz) sifted self-raising flour. Spoon into a greased and lined Swiss roll tin and bake for 10–12 mins in an oven heated to 200°C/400°F/Gas 6.

Scan with Smartphone
for shopping list

Time **1 hr 25 mins,
plus chilling**

Per portion
**314 Kcal
15.1g fat
(5.5g saturated)**

# Lemon meringue pie

Serves 6  Ⓥ

| | |
|---|---|
| **Plain flour** 225g (8oz) | **Caster sugar** 160g (5½oz) |
| **Salt** | **Large lemons** 2, grated zest and juice |
| **Butter** 125g (4½oz) | **Eggs** 3, separated |
| **Cornflour** 2 tbsp | |

1   Preheat the oven to 200°C/400°F/Gas 6. To make the pastry, sift the flour and salt into a bowl and add 110g (4oz) of the butter. Cut into the butter with a knife, then rub it in with your fingertips until the mixture looks like fine breadcrumbs. Sprinkle some cold water over the crumbs and mix to a stiff crumbly-looking paste with a round-ended knife, adding more water (you may need up to 3 tbsp) if necessary. To use a food processor, see step 2 of the quiche Lorraine on page 9.

2   Draw the pastry together with your fingertips and turn out onto a lightly floured work surface. Knead until smooth and then roll out to line a 20cm (8in) flan ring resting on a lightly greased baking sheet. Prick the base, line it with tin foil and bake for 15 minutes. Remove from the oven, lift out the tin foil and cook for a further 15 minutes or until crisp and golden. Remove from the oven and set aside. Reduce the oven temperature to 170°C/325°F/Gas 3.

3   To make the filling, put the cornflour, 50g (2oz) of the sugar and the lemon zest into a bowl. Mix together to a smooth paste with a little cold water. Warm 150ml (¼ pint) of water with the lemon juice in a saucepan. Combine with the lemon paste and then return to the pan. Cook, stirring, until the mixture comes to the boil. Reduce the heat and simmer for 3 minutes. Beat in the yolks and remaining butter. Cook for 1 minute, then pour into the flan case.

4   For the topping, whisk the egg whites with an electric hand whisk until they form stiff peaks. Continue whisking while gradually adding the remaining caster sugar. Spread over the filling and bake for 12–15 minutes until golden and the meringue is just set. Serve warm or cold.

157

Scan with Smartphone
for shopping list

Time 1½ hrs, plus chilling

Per portion
495 Kcal
37.3g fat
(21.4g saturated)

# Baked American cheesecake with autumn fruit sauce

Serves 10  Ⓥ Ⓕ

**For the cheesecake**

**Butter** 75g (3oz), melted

**Digestive biscuits** 150g (5oz), crushed

**Full fat soft cheese** 500g (1lb 2oz)

**Caster sugar** 110g (4oz)

**Vanilla bean paste** 2 tsp or 1 tsp **vanilla extract**

**Cornflour** 1 tbsp

**Eggs** 3

**Soured cream** 300ml pot

**Lemon juice** 1 tbsp

**Double cream** 150ml (¼ pint), whipped, to decorate

**Mixed fruit such as blackberries, raspberries and blackcurrants** 110g (4oz), to decorate

For the autumn fruit sauce

**Blackcurrants** 110g (4oz)

**Blackberries** 110g (4oz)

**Caster sugar** 50g (2oz) or to taste

**Cornflour** 2 tsp

1   Preheat the oven to 150°C/300°F/Gas 2. Grease and line a 20cm (8in) round deep loose-bottomed cake tin with a double thickness of greaseproof or non-stick baking paper. Stir the melted butter and crushed biscuits together and press evenly into the base.

2   Mix together the cheese, sugar, vanilla paste (or extract) and cornflour with a wooden spoon. Gradually beat in the eggs, one at a time, then fold in the soured cream and lemon juice. Spoon over the biscuit base and level the surface.

3   Set the cheesecake on a baking sheet and bake for 50–60 minutes until just set but still a bit wobbly. Turn off the oven and leave the cheesecake to cool in the oven to prevent it overcooking. Remove from the tin, set on a plate and chill for at least 4 hours.

4   For the sauce, put all the ingredients with 225ml (8fl oz) of water in a saucepan and bring to the boil, stirring constantly. Reduce the heat and simmer for 1–2 minutes, stirring. Cool slightly, then tip into a food processor and blend until smooth. Sieve to remove the pips. Taste and add sugar if necessary.

5 Spread the cream over the top of the cheesecake, followed by the fruit. Serve with the sauce.

Scan with Smartphone for shopping list

Time required
**20 mins**

Per portion
**343 Kcal**
**17.3g fat**
**(7.2g saturated)**

# Cinnamon & nutmeg spiced toast with cherry compote

Serves 4 Ⓥ

**For the cherry compote**

**Frozen dark sweet pitted cherries** 400g packet

**Cornflour** 1 tsp

**Caster sugar** 25g (1oz) or to taste

**Fresh orange juice** 2 tbsp

**For the spiced toast**

**Eggs** 3

**Ground nutmeg** 1 tsp

**Ground cinnamon** 1 tsp

**Ground cloves** a pinch

**Double cream** 2 tbsp, plus extra, whipped to serve (optional)

**White bread** 4 thick slices, crusts removed

**Butter** 25g (1oz)

**Sunflower oil** 1 tbsp

**Caster sugar** for sprinkling

1  Tip the frozen cherries into a saucepan and stir in all the remaining ingredients for the compote. Heat gently, stirring occasionally. Continue cooking until the cherries are heated through and the juices have thickened and there is no taste of cornflour.

2  Meanwhile, beat the eggs with the nutmeg, cinnamon, cloves and cream in a bowl and pour into a shallow dish. Lay the bread in the egg mix in a single layer and leave for a couple of minutes. Then turn the bread over so both sides are dipped in the egg and have absorbed a lot of the mix.

3  Heat the butter and oil in a large non-stick frying pan until the butter is foaming. Carefully lift the slices of bread out of the egg mix, place in the pan and cook in the hot oil until golden. Then, using a spatula, turn and cook again until crisp and golden.

4  Sprinkle a little caster sugar onto a plate. Turn the slices of toast in the sugar and cut into triangles. Serve with the cherry compote and some whipped cream, if using.

Scan with Smartphone for shopping list

**Cook's tip** The spices in this recipe will suit an adult taste but, if serving to children, you may like to use a little less.

Time **30 mins,
plus standing**

Per portion
**496 Kcal
39.8g fat
(19.8g saturated)**

# Cinnamon pancakes with rich orange butter

Serves 4 Ⓥ

For the batter
**Plain flour** 110g (4oz)
**Ground cinnamon** a generous pinch
**Eggs** 1 plus 1 yolk
**Milk** 150ml (¼ pint)
**Butter** 25g (1oz), melted
**Sunflower oil** for frying

For the rich orange butter
**Butter** 110g (4oz), softened
**Icing sugar** 25g (1oz), sifted
**Oranges 2,** grated zest only
**Cointreau** 1 tsp

1   Sift the flour into a bowl with the cinnamon. In a separate bowl, beat together the whole egg, egg yolk and milk and add 150ml (¼ pint) of water. Make a well in the centre of the flour and gradually whisk in the eggy milk to form a smooth batter. Add the melted butter, then cover with cling film and leave for 30 minutes.

2   For the rich orange butter, beat the butter until softened, then beat in the icing sugar and then the grated orange zest. Finally, beat in the Cointreau.

3   Heat a 23cm (9in) non-stick heavy-based frying pan and add a very small amount of the oil. Pour in enough batter to cover the base, swirling the pan. Cook until golden underneath and, using a palette knife, turn over the pancake and cook for another minute or so. Tip the pancake onto a plate and fold into quarters. Repeat with the rest of the batter until you have six to eight pancakes.

4   Melt half the orange butter in the pan over a gentle heat, then carefully add two to four of the folded pancakes (depending on how many you can cope with at once) and cook in the butter on both sides until golden and heated through. Repeat with the remaining pancakes, adding more orange butter as necessary. Serve with whipped cream.

163

Scan with Smartphone for shopping list

**Cook's tip** If you are making this for children, omit the ground cinnamon and Cointreau.

Time required
**1 hr**

Per portion
**207 Kcal**
**8.9g fat**
**(3.8g saturated)**

# Coffee soufflé

Serves 4 **Ⓥ**

**Butter** 15g (½oz), plus extra for greasing

**Caster sugar** 50g (2oz), plus 2 tsp extra for the soufflé dish

**Plain flour** 4 tbsp

**Milk** 150ml (¼ pint)

**Instant coffee granules** 1 tbsp

**Egg yolks** 3

**Egg whites** 4

**Icing sugar** to serve

1   Preheat the oven to 200°C/400°F/Gas 6. Butter a 1.25 litre (2 pint) soufflé dish and sprinkle 2 tsp of the caster sugar around the inside. Blend the flour with a little of the milk in a heatproof bowl to make a smooth paste.

2   Heat the remaining milk with the sugar in a saucepan over a gentle heat until it is hot, but not boiling. Remove the pan from the heat, add the coffee granules and stir to dissolve. Then pour onto the flour paste, stirring to mix.

3   Return the mixture to the saucepan and bring to the boil, stirring continuously. Cook for 2 minutes, stirring occasionally, until thickened. Remove the saucepan from the heat again, stir in the butter and leave to cool slightly before stirring in the egg yolks.

4   Whisk the egg whites with an electric hand whisk to stiff peaks and gently fold them into the coffee mixture with a metal spoon. Transfer to the prepared soufflé dish and bake for 35 minutes until well risen. Dust with icing sugar and serve at once in case the soufflé collapses.

165

Time required
1¼ hrs

Per portion
164 Kcal
7.7g fat
(2.9g saturated)

# Baked egg custard

Serves 4 **V**

**Eggs** 3, or 4 egg yolks          **Caster sugar** 25g (1oz)
**Milk** 600ml (1 pint)             **Ground nutmeg** for sprinkling

1   Preheat the oven to 170°C/325°F/Gas 3 and grease a 900ml
    (1½ pint) ovenproof dish. Beat the whole eggs or egg yolks with
    the milk and pour into the prepared dish. Stir in the sugar and
    sprinkle with nutmeg.

2   Stand the dish in a roasting tin containing enough hot water
    to come about half way up the sides of the dish. Bake the custard
    for 45 minutes–1 hour or until firm. Serve either hot or cold.

Time **45 mins**

Per portion
**221 Kcal**
**9.1g fat**
**(4.6g saturated)**

# Blueberry clafoutis

Serves 4 Ⓥ

**Fresh blueberries** 150g (5oz)

**Cornflour** 1 tsp

**Eggs** 2 medium

**Caster sugar** 50g (2oz)

**Butter** 25g (1oz), melted

**Plain flour** 50g (2oz)

**Milk** 225ml (8fl oz)

**Icing sugar** for dusting

1   Preheat the oven to 200°C/400°F/Gas 6 and thoroughly butter a 1.25 litre (2 pint) oval baking dish. Toss the blueberries in the cornflour and sprinkle over the base of the prepared baking dish.

2   Whisk together the eggs and sugar in a large bowl with an electric hand whisk until pale and thick. Pour in the melted butter, followed by the flour and milk, and whisk again until thoroughly combined.

3   Pour the batter over the blueberries and bake for 30–35 minutes or until golden and just set. Serve warm dusted with icing sugar.

**Cook's tip** If you don't have any blueberries to hand, use the same weight of fresh or frozen pitted cherries instead.

169

Time 1 hr 15 mins,
plus standing

Per portion
546 Kcal
28.2g fat
(16.5g saturated)

# Sticky toffee pudding

Serves 8  Ⓥ Ⓕ

**Chopped dates** 175g (6oz)
**Bicarbonate of soda** 1 tsp
**Butter** 50g (2oz), softened
**Soft light brown sugar** 175g (6oz)
**Eggs** 2 medium, beaten
**Self-raising flour** 175g (6oz)
**Vanilla ice cream** to serve (optional)

For the sauce
**Soft light brown sugar** 150g (5oz)
**Double cream** 150ml (¼ pint)
**Butter** 110g (4oz)

1   Preheat the oven to 180°C/350°F/Gas 4 and grease and line an 18cm (7in) square deep cake tin. Put the dates in a saucepan with 300ml (½ pint) of water and bring to the boil, then reduce the heat and simmer for 5 minutes, stirring occasionally. Remove the pan from the heat, add the bicarbonate of soda and leave to stand for 10 minutes.

2   Whisk the butter and sugar in a bowl with an electric hand whisk until soft and pale. Gradually add the eggs, whisking well after each addition. Fold in the flour. Then fold in the date mixture. Spoon into the prepared tin and bake for 40–50 minutes until the pudding has risen and is firm to the touch.

3   To make the sauce, put all the ingredients into a saucepan and heat gently until the sugar has dissolved, then bring to the boil. Reduce the heat and simmer for 1–2 minutes until the ingredients are combined and turned into a toffee sauce.

4   Cut the sticky pudding into portions and serve with the toffee sauce and a little vanilla ice cream, if using.

171

**Cook's tip** You can make this pudding in advance, then eat half of it and freeze the rest for another day. Leave to cool, wrap in cling film and freeze for up to a month. Thaw at room temperature for several hours, then warm through in the oven. You can't freeze the sauce so enjoy a little more.

Scan with Smartphone
for shopping list

| | |
|---|---|
| Executive Editor | Nick Rowe |
| Managing Editor | Emily Davenport |
| Editor | Emma Callery |
| Designer | Graham Meigh |
| Photographer | Steve Lee |
| Food Stylist | Sara Lewis |
| Props Stylist | Jo Harris |
| Recipes created by | Lucy Knox |
| Proof Reader | Aune Butt |
| Indexer | Christine Bernstein |
| Nutritional consultant | Dr Wendy Doyle |
| Recipe testers | Nathan Eardley |
| | Jamie Edgecombe |
| | Katy Hackforth |
| | Penny Meigh |
| | Claire Nadin |
| | Chris Perry |
| | Gudrun Waskett |
| Production | Teresa Wellborne |
| Special thanks | British Egg Information Service: |
| | Amanda Cryer |
| | Sara Emanuelson |
| For more detail on eggs visit | *www.britegg.co.uk* |

## For recipes and competitions visit

www.dairydiary.co.uk

dairydiary

@thedairydiary

www.dairydiarychat.co.uk

 like us on Facebook

Eaglemoss Consumer Publications Ltd
Electra House, Electra Way, Crewe, Cheshire, CW1 6WZ
Telephone 01270 270050
Website www.dairydiary.co.uk

First printed May 2012
© Eaglemoss Consumer Publications Ltd
ISBN-13: 978-0-9560894-8-9

123456789